EARTH

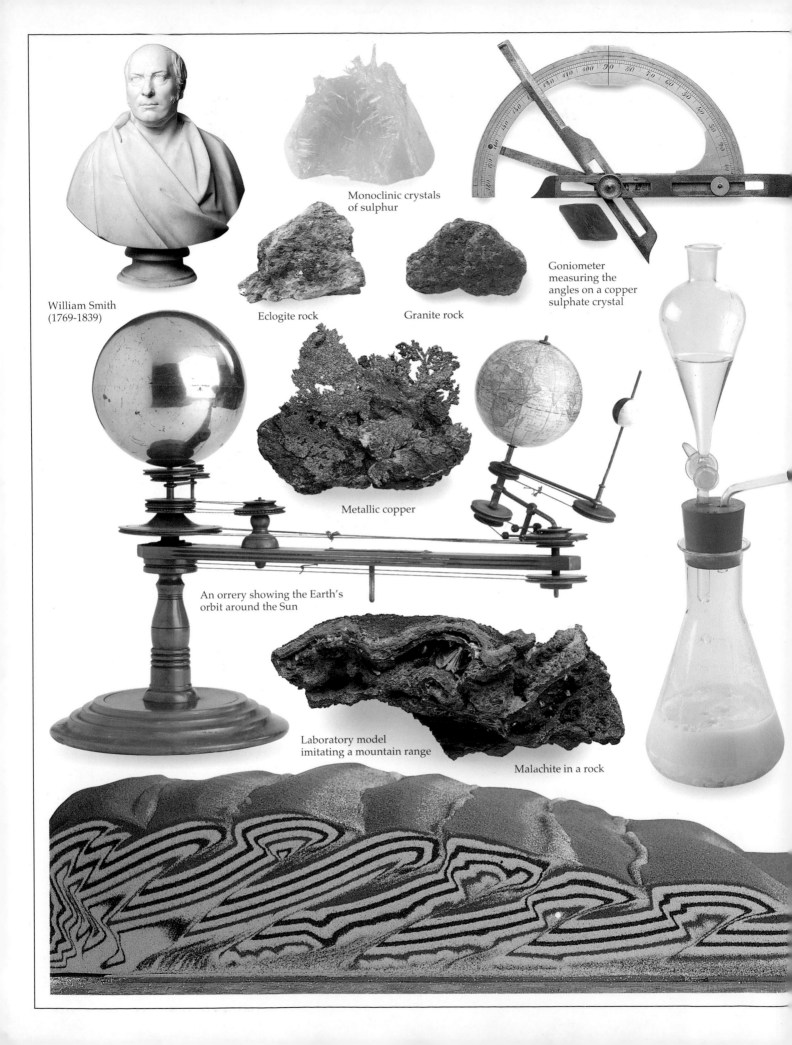

William Smith
(1769-1839)

Monoclinic crystals
of sulphur

Eclogite rock

Granite rock

Goniometer
measuring the
angles on a copper
sulphate crystal

Metallic copper

An orrery showing the Earth's
orbit around the Sun

Laboratory model
imitating a mountain range

Malachite in a rock

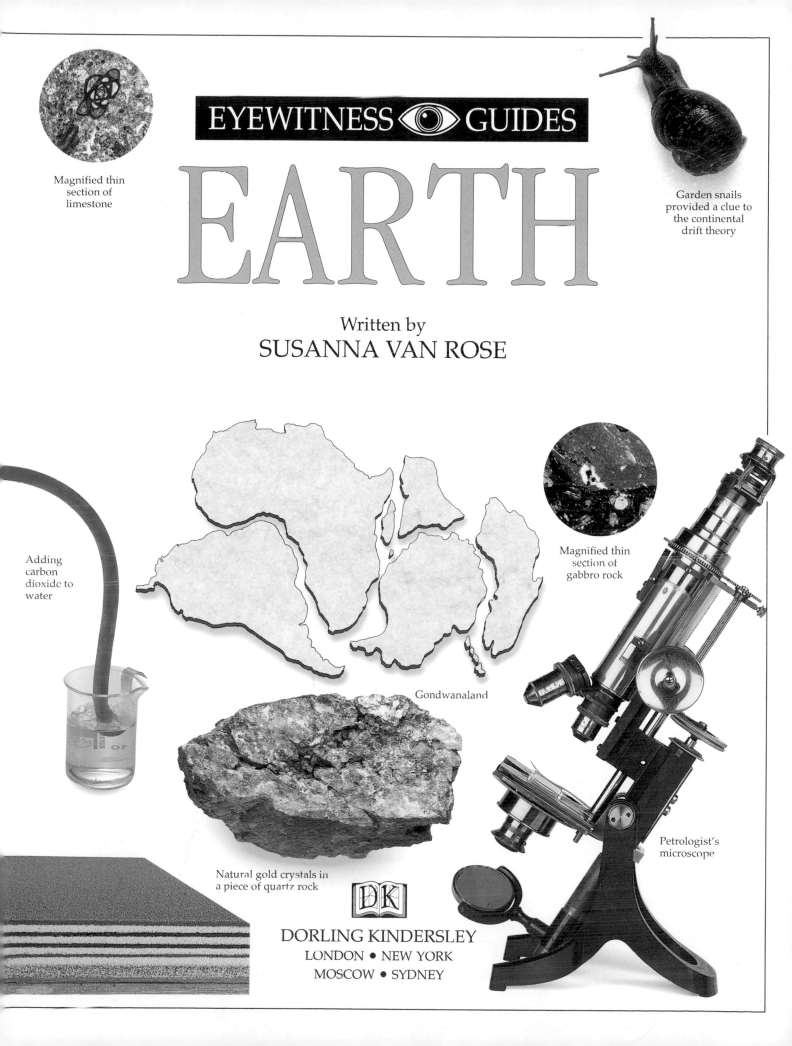

Magnified thin
section of
limestone

EYEWITNESS ◉ GUIDES

EARTH

Written by
SUSANNA VAN ROSE

Garden snails
provided a clue to
the continental
drift theory

Adding
carbon
dioxide to
water

Magnified thin
section of
gabbro rock

Gondwanaland

Natural gold crystals in
a piece of quartz rock

Petrologist's
microscope

DK

DORLING KINDERSLEY
LONDON • NEW YORK
MOSCOW • SYDNEY

Sieving fossils from sea floor sediments

A DORLING KINDERSLEY BOOK

Rapid cooling of heated sulphur

☞ **NOTE TO PARENTS AND TEACHERS**
The **Eyewitness Guides** series encourages children to observe and question the world around them. It will help families to answer their questions about why and how things work – from daily occurrences in the home to the mysteries of space. By regularly "looking things up" in these books, parents can promote reading for information every day.

At school, these books are a valuable resource. Teachers will find them especially useful for topic work in many subjects and can use the experiments and demonstrations in the books as inspiration for classroom activities and projects. **Eyewitness Guides** titles are also ideal reference books, providing a wealth of information about all areas of science within the curriculum. ☞

Heating powdered sulphur

Project Editor Charyn Jones
Art Editor Jane Bull
Design Assistant Helen Diplock
Production Adrian Gathercole
Special photography Clive Streeter
Picture Research Caroline Brooke
Managing Editor Josephine Buchanan
Managing Art Editor Lynne Brown
Editorial Consultant Dr John Cope,
UWCC, Wales

Powdered sulphur

Microscopic thin section of obsidian

This Eyewitness ®/™ Science book first published in Great Britain in 1994 by Dorling Kindersley Limited, 9 Henrietta Street, London WC2E 8PS

2 4 6 8 10 9 7 5 3 1

A CIP catalogue record for this book is available from the British Library

ISBN 0 7513 6138 0

Reproduced by Colourscan, Singapore
Printed in Singapore by
Toppan Printing Co. (S) Pte Ltd

A goniometer for measuring the angles of crystals

James Hutton (1726–1797)

A laboratory model of a delta

Contents

Samples collected by *Challenger* (1872-1875)

What makes up the Earth?

SATELLITE VIEW OF EARTH
The Earth is not exactly spherical in shape. It is flattened at the poles with a bulge at the equator so that the radius at the poles is 43 km (27 miles) shorter than the equatorial radius. The ancient Greek philosopher Pythagoras (*c.* 570-500 BC) thought that the Earth might be spherical in shape. This idea came to him as he watched ships approach from over the horizon. First he saw their masts; only as they came closer did the hulls appear.

As A SMALL PLANET in the vast Solar System, the Earth is unique in a number of ways. It has life, it has water, and it has a surface which is continually being renewed. This includes the thin rocky crust beneath our feet. The parts of the Earth that can be seen are just a tiny proportion of the whole planet. Beneath the crust lies the thick, many-layered mantle, which is also rocky, and at the centre there is a metal core, which is partly solid and partly liquid. The planet is surrounded by a magnetic field which fluctuates with time and blots out the intense radiations from the Sun which would be harmful to life. The rocky silicate crust is enveloped in a shroud of water and atmospheric gases (pp. 10-11) which have almost entirely come from the eruptions of volcanoes over time. The crust is made up of segments known as plates that move about slowly; over millions of years this movement changes the architecture of the continents as the plates interact (pp. 36-37).

EARLY COLLECTORS
Studying rocks in different places gives information about the huge variety of processes involved in the changing surface of the Earth. Mary Anning (b. 1799) was a fossil collector living in the west of England. She found fossils in ancient rock layers that had been exposed at the surface. This sort of information was used by her friend Sir Henry De La Beche (1796-1855), the English geologist who began systematic geological mapping and established the first national Geological Survey in Great Britain in 1835.

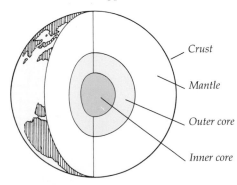

Crust

Mantle

Outer core

Inner core

THE INTERIOR OF THE EARTH
The Earth's crust is so thin that the line drawn here is too thick to be in scale. The crust is about 5 km (3 miles) thick under the oceans and 35 km (21 miles) thick under the continents. The underlying mantle is nearly 3,000 km (1,860 miles) thick. The metallic core has a liquid outer portion and a solid inner part. In the core, the pressure is something like a million times that of atmospheric pressure, while the temperature is around 4,500 °C (8,000 °F). It is impossible to simulate these conditions in a laboratory, so information about the metal that makes up the core is based on informed guesswork.

THE MAGNETIC FIELD
The liquid metallic outer core of the Earth flows and swirls, generating a magnetic field. From time to time – perhaps in thousands or tens of thousands of years – the direction of the field reverses, though it is not known how this happens. The lines of force of the magnetic field can be imagined as making great loops around the Earth between the north and south poles, and they act as a shield protecting the Earth from the energetic flood of electrically charged particles coming from the Sun that are known as the solar wind. (This shield creates a magnetic cavity known as the magnetosphere.) When the Earth's magnetic field meets up with the solar wind, the Earth's magnetic field is compressed on the side nearest to the Sun. On the far side it makes a trailing edge. The wire model shows the pattern made by the interaction of the solar wind with the Earth's magnetic field.

Magnetosphere

Magnetotail

Magnet field compressed

Direction of solar wind

Earth

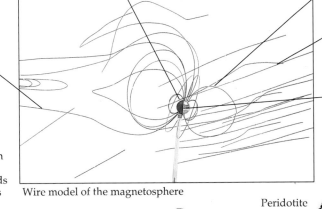

Wire model of the magnetosphere

Peridotite rock

The Earth's ingredients

Apart from water, air, and rocks, finding out what the rest of the Earth is made up of is not always possible (pp. 40-41). Some upper mantle rocks are seen at the surface in volcanic eruptions of magma (p. 25). These give clues to the composition of the mantle. It is even more difficult to imagine the conditions of the highly compressed metal at the Earth's solid core. This the densest part of the Earth because it is under huge pressure.

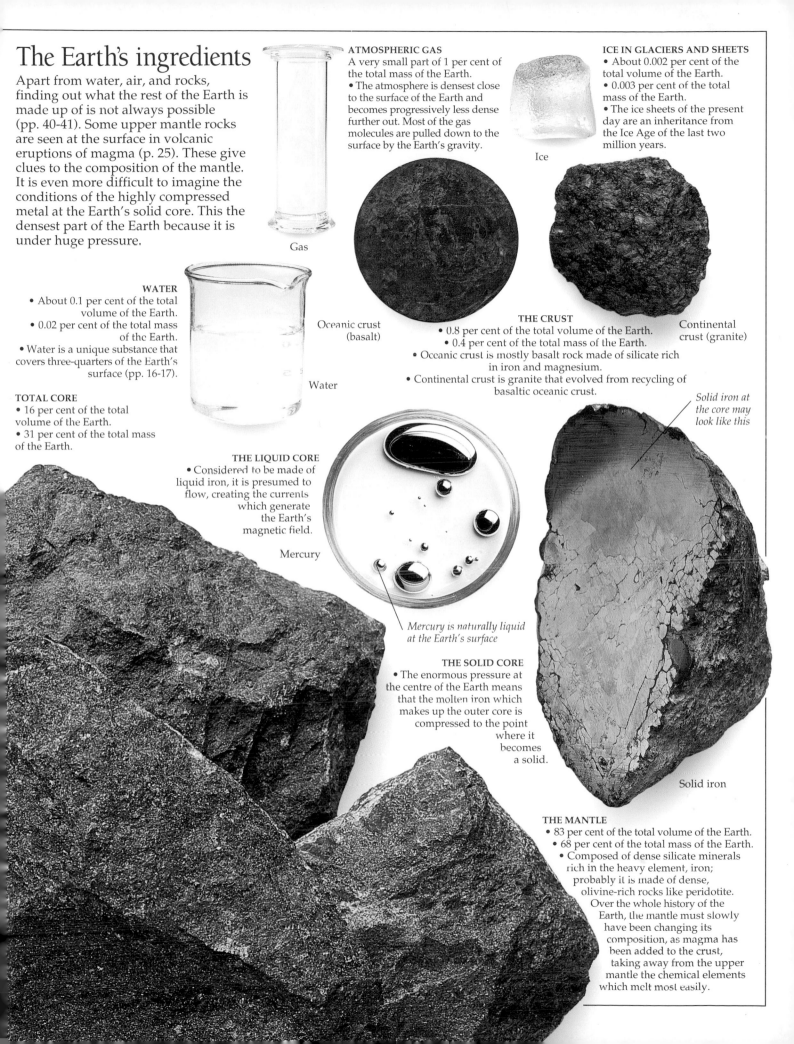

Gas

ATMOSPHERIC GAS
A very small part of 1 per cent of the total mass of the Earth.
• The atmosphere is densest close to the surface of the Earth and becomes progressively less dense further out. Most of the gas molecules are pulled down to the surface by the Earth's gravity.

ICE IN GLACIERS AND SHEETS
• About 0.002 per cent of the total volume of the Earth.
• 0.003 per cent of the total mass of the Earth.
• The ice sheets of the present day are an inheritance from the Ice Age of the last two million years.

Ice

Oceanic crust (basalt)

WATER
• About 0.1 per cent of the total volume of the Earth.
• 0.02 per cent of the total mass of the Earth.
• Water is a unique substance that covers three-quarters of the Earth's surface (pp. 16-17).

Water

THE CRUST
• 0.8 per cent of the total volume of the Earth.
• 0.4 per cent of the total mass of the Earth.
• Oceanic crust is mostly basalt rock made of silicate rich in iron and magnesium.
• Continental crust is granite that evolved from recycling of basaltic oceanic crust.

Continental crust (granite)

TOTAL CORE
• 16 per cent of the total volume of the Earth.
• 31 per cent of the total mass of the Earth.

THE LIQUID CORE
• Considered to be made of liquid iron, it is presumed to flow, creating the currents which generate the Earth's magnetic field.

Mercury

Mercury is naturally liquid at the Earth's surface

Solid iron at the core may look like this

THE SOLID CORE
• The enormous pressure at the centre of the Earth means that the molten iron which makes up the outer core is compressed to the point where it becomes a solid.

Solid iron

THE MANTLE
• 83 per cent of the total volume of the Earth.
• 68 per cent of the total mass of the Earth.
• Composed of dense silicate minerals rich in the heavy element, iron; probably it is made of dense, olivine-rich rocks like peridotite. Over the whole history of the Earth, the mantle must slowly have been changing its composition, as magma has been added to the crust, taking away from the upper mantle the chemical elements which melt most easily.

Early ideas about the Earth

MANY EARLY CONCEPTS about the origin and make-up of the Earth were well founded in observation and reason; others were long-held traditions. Sometimes there is a connection between traditional ideas and scientific thought. At other times, it is hard to see any relationship. The development of knowledge and understanding about our surroundings has not always followed a straight line. Although the ancient Greeks and Egyptians established that the Earth was round and calculated its radius extraordinarily accurately, many centuries later some people still believed that the Earth was flat. Early maps were made of local areas and were drawn on flat cloth, so the idea of a flat Earth was a logical extension of the flat-map representation. Early explorers, some of them careful observers, travelled extensively and extended knowledge about coastlines and new lands and oceans. In the 18th century one of the earliest modern geologists, James Hutton (1726-1797), put forward pioneering ideas about Earth processes. Leaving aside inherited ideas, he worked from observation.

MAP OF THE WORLD
This map of the world (*mappa mundi*) was drawn in the 10th century AD as part of the initial letter on the page of an illuminated manuscript.

TWELFTH-CENTURY MAPPA MUNDI
Early maps contained pictures as well as abstract representations of the landscape. These pictures were sometimes of the gods, or drawings of the places to be found on the route. This map features mountains and rivers and covers the area from Babylonia (present-day Iraq) to Caledonia (present-day Scotland).

Mountain

River

DIVINING TWIG
Finding underground water with forked twigs is a method that is still used today in places. The twig is stretched out taut in the diviner's hands. For diviners, it twists violently when it is carried over the underground water.

JAMES HUTTON
Hutton was a Scottish geologist whose interest in agriculture led him to study the fertility of soil. This led him to more wide-ranging observations of the surrounding Scottish countryside. His Plutonist ideas about the origins of rocks being related to volcanic activity came from studies of the volcanic rocks in Edinburgh. This contradicted the Neptunists who held different views about the origin of rocks (p. 22). It was Hutton's work that gave the first hints of the immensity of geological time.

IN SEARCH OF METALS
Divining the landscape, whether for water, for minerals, or for auspicious sites, is even followed today in some technological societies. In his book, *De Re Metallica*, Georg Bauer, a German doctor, philosopher, and mineralogist known as Agricola (1494-1555), describes the physical properties of minerals, where metals are found, and how to extract them. He also illustrated the use of forked twigs. He remained sceptical about the usefulness of divination, but admitted that some people were successful with the method.

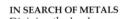

The diviner

Small hand axe

Flaked cutting edge

Large hand axe

THE STONE AGE

When people first learned to use the materials from which the Earth is made, stone was their first choice. Some rock types were more suitable than others; they could be worked to a sharp edge which lasted, even in heavy use such as felling trees. Not all rocks were suitable for making tools. Some rocks could not be sharpened; other rocks were too weak to retain the sharp edge.

Cutting edge used for cutting plants and wood and skinning animals

DIVINING LANDSCAPE

Feng shui is the ancient Chinese practice of landscape divining. The landscape is believed to contain hidden energy. Feng shui sees rounded hills as having female characteristics (yin) and rugged mountains as having male characteristics (yang). Along with other elements, such as fire and water, these must all be balanced if there is to be harmony and prosperity.

The compass is consulted

Ch'ing dynasty painting showing feng shui compass in use

CHINESE COMPASS

The origins of the feng shui compass are unclear. It may have developed from a simple diviner's board which was used for direction finding, or its origin may be connected with the chess board, as pieces were thrown on to the board as dice. The name feng shui means wind and water. In Hong Kong, the feng shui diviner is still consulted before any building of significance is built or bought. This ensures that the site, the architectural style, and the purpose of the building are in harmony.

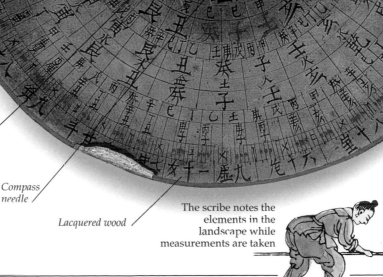

Inner ring with heavenly trigrams

Compass needle

Lacquered wood

The scribe notes the elements in the landscape while measurements are taken

BRINGING HARMONY

Many satisfying buildings throughout the world follow the principles of feng shui. According to feng shui, straight lines are bad because they allow energy to rush too forcefully through the landscape for its beneficial powers to be used. A winding pathway or an undulating wall, as here at Chengde in China, brings better harmony with the universe.

A cocoon of gas

THE OUTERMOST PART OF THE EARTH is its shroud of gas, the atmosphere. It extends out at least 1,000 km (600 miles) above the solid surface of the Earth, but three-quarters of this life-sustaining atmosphere is concentrated in the lowest 10 km (6 miles). The atmosphere is a mixture of different gases which together make up air. The most abundant gas in the lower atmosphere is nitrogen, which makes up 78 per cent. Oxygen, so vital in supporting animal life on Earth, makes up less than 20 per cent. Carbon dioxide, just a small fraction of the total atmosphere, is vital in sustaining plant life, and it plays a role in keeping the temperature of the atmosphere steady. Tiny traces of other gases – argon and neon – are clues to the origin of the Earth's atmosphere. The Earth's atmosphere has mostly come from gases spewed out by volcanoes since the Earth began, although some, like oxygen, are a later contribution from plant life. The layer of the atmosphere closest to the land is called the troposphere. Here, temperature and humidity change rapidly, and the air is turbulent, thus creating weather patterns.

PERPETUAL BLACK SKY
The Moon has no atmosphere surrounding it. This makes its sky black, because there are no atmospheric gases to trap and scatter sunlight which would give a blue or white sky. Lack of atmospheric gases also means that the Moon has no weather.

Paralvinella

UNSEEING CREATURES
Some creatures on the Earth exist without atmospheric oxygen. Blind and living in the perpetual darkness of the deep ocean, these sulphide worms have developed an alternative body chemistry to cope with their environment. They get their energy supply from sulphide minerals oozing from hot springs on the ocean floor (p. 38) where temperatures reach 270 ºC (518 ºF). Bacteria living nearby take dissolved carbon dioxide from the ocean water and build organic molecules using the hydrogen sulphide from the mineral springs.

Carbon dioxide

Argon and others

Oxygen

Nitrogen

GASES IN THE ATMOSPHERE
The Earth's atmosphere is unique. If it had formed from gases which are abundant in the Solar System, the Earth would have an atmosphere made up mostly of hydrogen and helium, with some methane and ammonia. Instead, processes such as the evolution of bacterial life forms and plants have created an atmosphere dominated by nitrogen. Another feature of the Earth's atmosphere is that most of its argon is Ar40 (argon 40), from radioactive decay of potassium 40, whereas gases in the solar system are dominated by Ar36 and Ar38.

GREEN SLIME
Oxygen is a relative newcomer in the Earth's atmosphere. It has come from plants which, during photosynthesis, use carbon dioxide to make their food, giving out oxygen. The earliest photosynthesizing plants probably looked like these algae, which today grow in hot volcanic springs. Once the algae had evolved, about 3,600 million years ago, they began slowly to add oxygen to the atmosphere.

THE ATMOSPHERE FROM SPACE

Viewed from space, the Earth looks totally unlike all the other planets. It is partly shrouded in white clouds, which swirl in patterns, making weather. The gravity fields of the small planetary bodies cannot hold on to lightweight molecules of gas, so the Moon, Mercury, and Mars have little atmosphere. Venus, being larger, holds an atmosphere rich in carbon dioxide.

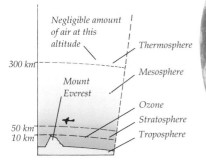

LAYERS OF ATMOSPHERE

The Earth's atmosphere has several layers. The heights of these layers vary with season, latitude, and time. Weather is confined to the troposphere, and almost all clouds are below this level. In the stratosphere lies the important ozone layer that filters the Sun's rays.

AURORA AUSTRALIS

Within the thermosphere, 300 km (190 miles) up, electrons and protons thrown off by the Sun interact with particles to produce a shimmering light effect. This is mostly seen at polar latitudes. This aurora australis, in the southern hemisphere, was photographed from the space shuttle *Discovery* in 1991.

BANDED IRON

Between about 3,000 and 2,000 million years ago, layers of red and black striped rocks were formed that rarely occur later on in the Earth's history. These are the banded iron formations, where the iron has reacted chemically with oxygen to form oxides. During the time these formed, they must have used up huge amounts of oxygen from the oceanic waters. This proves that, at this time, algae (p. 10) were rapidly increasing in numbers, making the oceans steadily more oxygen rich. Oxygen began to escape into the atmosphere as red iron oxide sediments accumulated on land.

Red hematite (an iron oxide)

Black hematite (an iron oxide)

FERTILE LAND

The diversity of life that flourishes on the Earth is unique. The Earth's atmosphere gives some protection from radiations from space. Its gases provide nourishment for both plants and animals. Winds in the troposphere and ocean currents moderate temperatures through what would otherwise be scorching day and freezing night.

Climate in the past

THE ROLE OF THE SUN
In 1941 the Croatian meteorologist Milutin Milankovitch suggested that changes in the Earth's orbit around the Sun caused long-term changes in climate. He spent many years working out how much radiation from the Sun had been received at different latitudes over the last 650,000 years to help prove his theories.

THE EARTH'S CLIMATE HAS CHANGED enormously over geological time. The shapes of the continents have altered and they have moved around relative to the equator and to the poles (pp. 36-37). To find out about these changes, geologists look into the rocks and read them as a kind of history book, going back 4,000 million years. The rocks show that places now far from the equator have had baking deserts at times in the past, and that tropical coral reefs flourished on shorelines of what is now Europe. The positions of the continents have an effect on the movement of air masses and on weather patterns. When all the continents were together as Pangaea (pp. 34-35), not much rain fell in the interior, which was largely a desert. The rocks also show that in the last 2 million years glaciers covered large parts of the world (pp. 58-59). Another reason for climate change is the position of the Earth in its orbit in relation to the Sun.

CHANGING POSITIONS
The Earth's orbit is an ellipse – it is sometimes more circular, and sometimes less circular, so that the distance of the Earth from the Sun varies. The changing positions of the Sun and the Moon give an uneven pull on the Earth's bulging equator. So 11,000 years ago, the northern hemisphere, which then was thick with glacier ice, was nearest the Sun in summer, encouraging the glaciers to melt, helping to bring an end to the Ice Age.

Impression of shell

Earth

Moon

Rock from Mt Snowdon, Wales

Sun

Distance from the Sun to the Earth varies over 100,000-year cycle

An orrery to show planetary motions

CONTINENTAL HISTORY
Fossils tell us about climate and environment in the past. Sea shells found in rocks of high mountains show that marine sediment deposits have been uplifted to form high plateaux and mountain ranges (pp. 46-49). The fossil plant *Glossopteris* is found in rocks 350-200 million years old within each of the southern hemisphere continents. This, along with other evidence, indicates that all these land masses must have been joined together during this time.

ICE-AGE LEGACY
The five Great Lakes of North America owe their origin to changes in glacier ice over the last 14,000 years. The huge weight of the thick sheet of ice pushed down the surface of the land underneath, making a low area. This low region persisted long after the glaciers had melted; the rock was slow to bounce back on release of the pressure (pp. 40-41). As the glacier ice melted, it provided thousands of years' worth of fresh meltwater, which ponded into lakes on the low land.

Lake Michigan   *Lake Huron*   *Lake Erie*

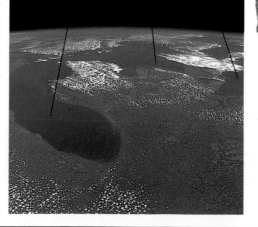

Glossopteris leaf

Straight leaf margin

Shale rock from India

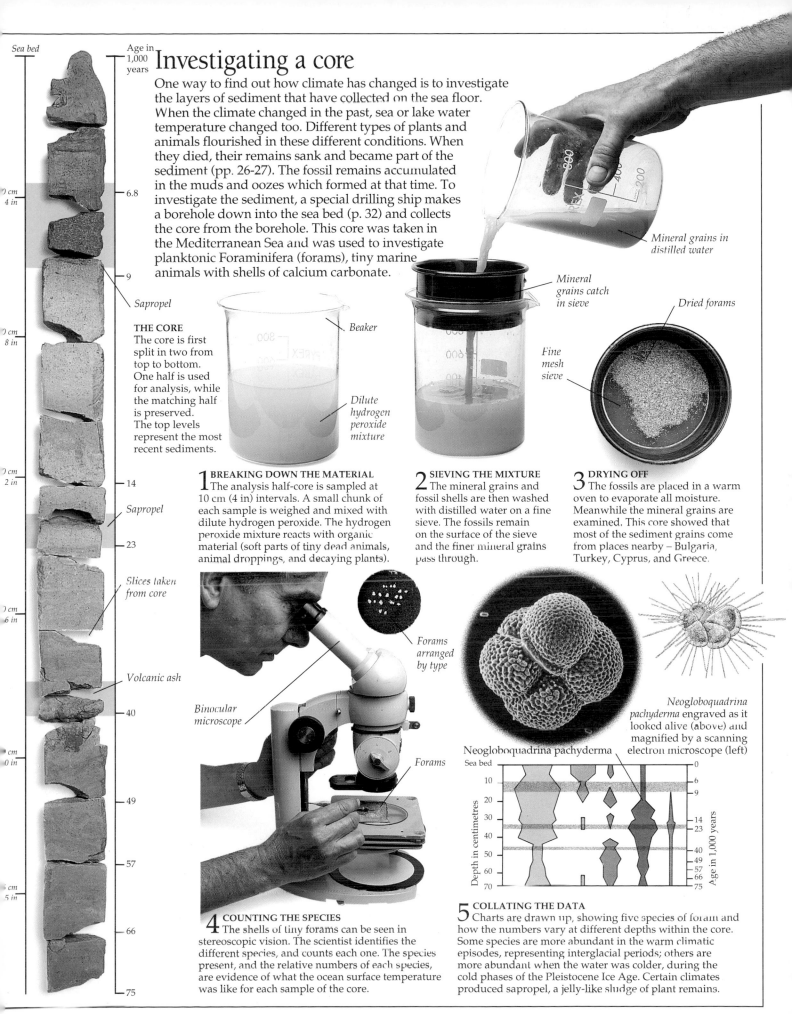

Investigating a core

One way to find out how climate has changed is to investigate the layers of sediment that have collected on the sea floor. When the climate changed in the past, sea or lake water temperature changed too. Different types of plants and animals flourished in these different conditions. When they died, their remains sank and became part of the sediment (pp. 26-27). The fossil remains accumulated in the muds and oozes which formed at that time. To investigate the sediment, a special drilling ship makes a borehole down into the sea bed (p. 32) and collects the core from the borehole. This core was taken in the Mediterranean Sea and was used to investigate planktonic Foraminifera (forams), tiny marine animals with shells of calcium carbonate.

Sea bed

Age in 1,000 years

6.8

Sapropel

9

THE CORE
The core is first split in two from top to bottom. One half is used for analysis, while the matching half is preserved. The top levels represent the most recent sediments.

Mineral grains in distilled water

Mineral grains catch in sieve

Dried forams

Beaker

Fine mesh sieve

Dilute hydrogen peroxide mixture

14

Sapropel

23

1 BREAKING DOWN THE MATERIAL
The analysis half-core is sampled at 10 cm (4 in) intervals. A small chunk of each sample is weighed and mixed with dilute hydrogen peroxide. The hydrogen peroxide mixture reacts with organic material (soft parts of tiny dead animals, animal droppings, and decaying plants).

2 SIEVING THE MIXTURE
The mineral grains and fossil shells are then washed with distilled water on a fine sieve. The fossils remain on the surface of the sieve and the finer mineral grains pass through.

3 DRYING OFF
The fossils are placed in a warm oven to evaporate all moisture. Meanwhile the mineral grains are examined. This core showed that most of the sediment grains come from places nearby – Bulgaria, Turkey, Cyprus, and Greece.

Slices taken from core

Volcanic ash

40

Binocular microscope

Forams arranged by type

Forams

Neogloboquadrina pachyderma engraved as it looked alive (above) and magnified by a scanning electron microscope (left)

Neogloboquadrina pachyderma

49

57

66

75

4 COUNTING THE SPECIES
The shells of tiny forams can be seen in stereoscopic vision. The scientist identifies the different species, and counts each one. The species present, and the relative numbers of each species, are evidence of what the ocean surface temperature was like for each sample of the core.

5 COLLATING THE DATA
Charts are drawn up, showing five species of foram and how the numbers vary at different depths within the core. Some species are more abundant in the warm climatic episodes, representing interglacial periods; others are more abundant when the water was colder, during the cold phases of the Pleistocene Ice Age. Certain climates produced sapropel, a jelly-like sludge of plant remains.

Sea bed

Depth in centimetres — 10, 20, 30, 40, 50, 60, 70

Age in 1,000 years — 6, 9, 14, 23, 40, 49, 57, 66, 75

13

Watery planet

OVER THREE-QUARTERS of the Earth's surface is covered by water – it would be more logical to call the planet "Water" instead of "Earth". Even with the continents scattered around as they are today, one great ocean dominates half the globe. Of the rain that falls on the land, just over one-third runs off into rivers and is quickly returned to the sea. The other two-thirds soaks into the soil and underlying rock and remains for years or even tens of thousands of years as ground water. It is ground water that nourishes springs and wells, and keeps rivers flowing in times of drought. All water is involved in a never-ending flow from ocean to atmosphere to rivers to underground rocks, always returning eventually to the ocean. This great journey is called the water cycle. Understanding the way in which water moves from one place to another is the study of hydrology, and someone who looks specifically at the movement of underground water is a hydrogeologist.

BLUE PLANET
Viewed from a satellite above the Pacific Ocean, the Earth appears to be almost completely covered in water. A few chains of islands dot the watery surface. The Pacific is so big that all the land area of the Earth could be fitted into it. The oceans are much deeper on average than the land is high.

Pacific Ocean

Water evaporates from forests, fields, lakes, and rivers to become clouds

Clouds rise and cool over land, and drop moisture as rain or snow

Some water runs over the surface of the ground into rivers and lakes

Water evaporates from oceans to form clouds

Some water soaks into the ground and moves slowly back to the ocean

WATER CYCLE
Water is a fluid continually moving from one place to another. It does this partly by changing from liquid to vapour and back again. The Sun's heat warms the ocean water near the surface, and some molecules of water are heated enough to evaporate (p. 16). These energetic molecules escape from the ocean and become water vapour which collects in clouds. When clouds are cooled, they can no longer hold water as vapour, so drops condense and fall as rain and snow. Because of the distribution of land and ocean, most rain falls straight back into the ocean to repeat the cycle. Some rain falls on land and is used by plants and animals. Some gathers in lakes and rivers, only to run downhill into the ocean once more. Some rainfall over land takes longer to return to the ocean; it travels slowly through tiny pores and cracks in underground rocks.

QUANTITIES OF WATER
Most of the world's water is salty. Less than 6 per cent accounts for all the fresh water in rivers and lakes, the water underground in rocks, and the moisture in the atmosphere. Some fresh water is temporarily locked up in ice caps and glaciers. Since the end of the last Ice Age this has been melting and has raised global sea level by tens of metres. If the world climate continues to warm, over the next hundreds or thousands of years the remaining ice could melt and raise global sea level by a few more tens of metres.

Ocean water 94%

Ground water 4.34%

Ice caps and glaciers 1.65%

Rivers and lakes 0.01%

Water vapour

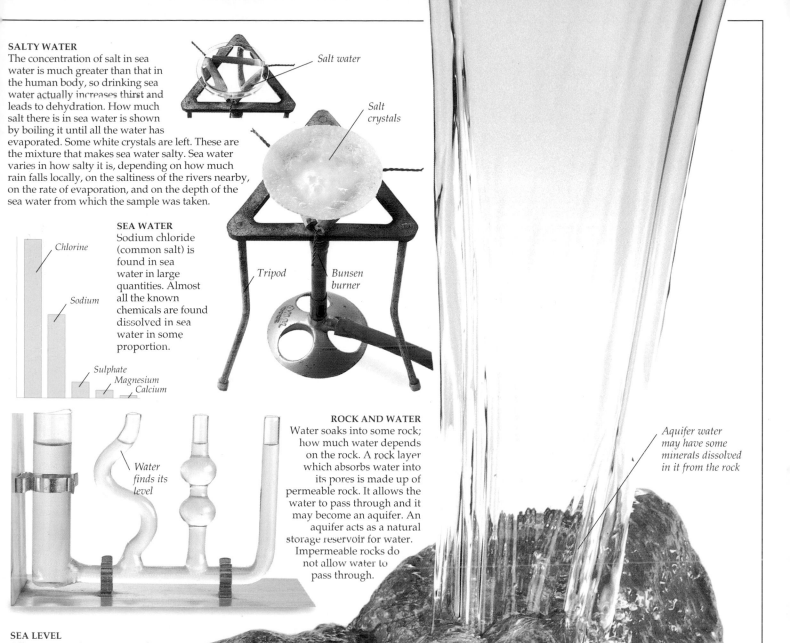

SALTY WATER

The concentration of salt in sea water is much greater than that in the human body, so drinking sea water actually increases thirst and leads to dehydration. How much salt there is in sea water is shown by boiling it until all the water has evaporated. Some white crystals are left. These are the mixture that makes sea water salty. Sea water varies in how salty it is, depending on how much rain falls locally, on the saltiness of the rivers nearby, on the rate of evaporation, and on the depth of the sea water from which the sample was taken.

Salt water

Salt crystals

SEA WATER

Sodium chloride (common salt) is found in sea water in large quantities. Almost all the known chemicals are found dissolved in sea water in some proportion.

Tripod

Bunsen burner

Chlorine

Sodium

Sulphate

Magnesium

Calcium

Water finds its level

ROCK AND WATER

Water soaks into some rock; how much water depends on the rock. A rock layer which absorbs water into its pores is made up of permeable rock. It allows the water to pass through and it may become an aquifer. An aquifer acts as a natural storage reservoir for water. Impermeable rocks do not allow water to pass through.

Aquifer water may have some minerals dissolved in it from the rock

SEA LEVEL

All oceans are interconnected, so sea level is fairly constant all the way round the Earth. This is because, being a liquid, water flows downhill to the lowest place, and then finds its level in a local area. Inland seas and lakes are not connected to the world oceans, so their levels may vary widely. Some are above global sea level, others, such as the Dead Sea in Israel, are below it. Differences in gravity and changes in atmospheric pressure and the tides cause bulges and depressions in the surface of the oceans.

The properties of water

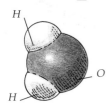

WATER IS AN UNUSUAL LIQUID because of the way its molecules are bonded together. One effect of this bonding is the unusual density of water. Most substances occupy a smaller space – they become more dense – as they are cooled. However, water is most dense at 4 °C (39.2 °F). Below that temperature, its density becomes less. Ice at 0 °C (32 °F) is less dense than water at 0 °C. This is why ice floats on water. Water takes a huge amount of heat to transform it from its liquid state into a gas, and from its solid state, ice, into a liquid. The equable temperature on the Earth is largely maintained by these unusual characteristics of water. Water also has high surface tension, which helps in making raindrops in the atmosphere, and in the way water is able to travel through rocks and soil. Water is a solvent; it dissolves a great many substances relatively easily. Its ability to do this affects how rocks are weathered (pp. 50-51), as some of the chemical elements which make up rocks go into solution during weathering.

UNITS OF WATER
Water is made up of two elements – oxygen and hydrogen. Its molecules bind together to form aggregates of water molecules, with a special bond called the hydrogen bond. This causes the molecules to join together, so that at room temperature, water forms droplets rather than floating around as a gas.

MAKING RAINDROPS
The surface tension of water is the ability of the surface to shrink and "wrap around" the water so that it holds the contents together. The clingy wetness of water is also a result of the surface tension. The force of the surface pulling to hold the water together is enough to allow water to soak up and wet a towel or filter paper when they are dipped into the water.

Solid

Liquid

Water molecule (H₂O)

Gas

SOLID, LIQUID, AND GAS
Most substances pack together into a regular arrangement when they are in a solid state. As a liquid, the ordered arrangement breaks down, and the molecules are more spaced out. With more heat, the spacing gets greater, until eventually molecules are so far apart that the substance becomes a gas. As water is cooled to 4 °C (39.2 °F), or cold water is heated to 4 °C, the molecules pack together in a more economical way, so that they occupy less space. This gives water its maximum density at this temperature.

Water remains in droplets

WATER BOATMAN
When a water boatman (*Dolomedes fimbriatus*) lands on a pond, its weight and the way it is distributed over the feet is less than the pulling-together effect of water's surface tension, so the boatman floats. The water surface curves down around its feet. This surface tension effect is how water wets things. As its surface pulls together, it surrounds fibres or grains of rock or soil with which it comes into contact.

Egg sinks in tap water

Egg floats in salty water

Curve on surface of water

Green dye added to water

CAPILLARY ACTION
If a thin tube stands upright in water, the water will rise up inside the tube. There is an upward curve of the water surface where the water touches the tube. The thinner the tube, the higher the water rises, as surface tension pulls the curved surface together. Water soaks into soil and rocks and moves down under the force of gravity. However, water also travels up through rocks by this capillary action. The curved surface always pulls together as the water envelops each tiny grain of rock in turn. Water can therefore be drawn up through soil and rock and evaporated at the surface (p. 14).

FLOATING EGGS
The density of water changes when it has salt dissolved in it. An egg sinks in fresh water, which means the egg has a density greater than that of the water. Salty water is more dense than fresh water, and when the amount of saltiness – the salinity – is high enough, the egg floats. The varying density of sea water is one of the factors that drives the water currents that circulate water in the oceans.

Weight

MEASURING DENSITY
A hydrometer is an instrument that measures the density of a liquid. It is floated upright in the liquid, sinking more deeply into less dense liquids. Weights are attached to it and the reading taken. This one was used to measure the alcohol content of drinks for assessing the amount of tax payable.

Flotation bulb

Acid

Hydrometer

LIMESTONE CAVES
The hydrogen and oxygen that go to make up water are bonded together in such a way that the molecule has a positive charge at one end and a negative charge at the other. This makes it easy for water to attract other charged substances, and it does this by dissolving them. It dissolves the rock limestone to make caves. Later, the dissolved chemicals may become stalagmites and stalactites (p. 51).

Limestone caves at Lascaux in France

Carbon dioxide gas is given off

ACID RAIN
Pure water is neither acid nor alkaline. Indicator paper held in pure or distilled water shows that it is neutral. Rainwater is always acid, because it contains carbon dioxide. As raindrops fall through the atmosphere, they dissolve some carbon dioxide from the air. This makes the rain a weak acid. In this experiment, carbon dioxide gas is made by adding acid to calcium carbonate chips. The gas is passed into distilled water, which then becomes acid as shown by the indicator paper. Acid rainwater is a weathering agent; it can dissolve limestone – although slowly.

Indicator paper shows neutral

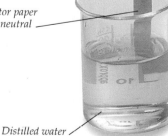

Indicator paper shows slight acidity

Distilled water

Calcium carbonate chips

Carbonic acid

Realms of ice

MANY OF THE WORLD'S HIGH MOUNTAIN RANGES still have glaciers (pp. 58-59). Both glaciers and ice sheets were much more extensive during the cold glacial phases of the last two million years. Now the Earth is believed to be in an interglacial period with Greenland and Antarctica the only extensively ice-covered lands – leftovers from the last cold phase. The Antarctic ice sheet probably came into existence 35 million years ago when Antarctica broke away from the other land masses (pp. 30-31). This allowed free circulation of oceanic currents around Antarctica, isolating it from the warmth of the tropical oceanic waters (p. 33). The water to make ice comes from snow which falls and is compacted. This snow comes from water vapour evaporated from the oceans (p. 14), so sea level drops. When glaciers and ice sheets melt, sea level rises again.

LOUIS AGASSIZ (1807-1873)
In 1837 Swiss zoologist Agassiz put forward the idea that northern Europe had once been covered with glaciers. They had carried the boulders which littered the Swiss mountain valleys, made of rocks similar to those rock types found higher up the valleys.

Arctic ice   Greenland

Antarctica

POLAR ICE
The South Pole is surrounded by thick ice which covers the continent of Antarctica to an average depth of 2.5 km (1½ miles). A small fraction of the Antarctic ice sheet extends beyond the land and floats on the Antarctic Ocean. By contrast, the North Pole has no land. It is a floating mass of sea ice – it is possible to travel by submarine to the North Pole under this sea ice.

ICEBERGS
Icebergs are made of freshwater ice brought into the sea by the break-up of glaciers, or when chunks calve off from the floating part of an ice sheet. A small part of the ice floats above the salty sea water (p. 15), the vast bulk being unseen below. As icebergs are derived from land, they contain boulders and rock fragments which the glacier or ice sheet has plucked from the solid rock. The rock makes the icebergs heavy so they float even lower in the sea. Most Antarctic icebergs originate from the floating ice surrounding the continent.

SEA ICE
Exploring the polar regions means braving the sea ice and icebergs. Polar ships follow the open water "leads" through the icescape. Their hulls are specially strengthened to help batter their way through, and also to protect them from crushing if the ice should freeze around them. The floating ice of both hemispheres is called pack ice. The amount varies from summer to winter.

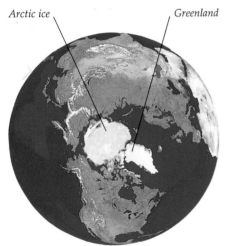

The birth of an iceberg

Chemicals for use
with rock specimens

*Cupel with spirit
burner for heating
chemicals*

SCOTT THE SCIENTIST
Captain Robert Scott (1868-1912) died returning from
his trek to the South Pole. He is less well-known for his
scientific work during the trip. His equipment included
this portable chemistry laboratory which enabled him
to work on the rock samples collected by the
expedition as he travelled.

FOSSIL LOBSTER
Although Antarctica is
98 per cent covered by ice, geologists
have mapped its rocks. Fossil plants such as
Glossopteris (p. 12) have been found, and more
recently many crustacean fossils have been uncovered, some
of which are new species not found elsewhere. This fossil lobster
from Upper Cretaceous rocks is about 80 million years old.

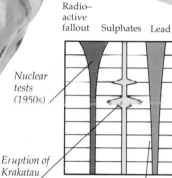

Radio–
active
fallout   Sulphates   Lead

Present
day

*Nuclear
tests
(1950s)*

*Eruption of
Krakatau
(1883)*

*Industrial
revolution (1750)*

Time in 30 year cycles

ANALYZING ICE CORES
This ice core was drilled
from the polar ice sheet
and returned to the
laboratory for tests.
Minute amounts are
taken at regular intervals
and analyzed to find
out more about the
atmosphere and climate
of the past, just like a
sediment core from
the Mediterranean is
analyzed (p. 13). The ice
is melted naturally in
sterile conditions so that
no pollutants from the
new environment can
contaminate it. The
results are collated into
a chart to show the
levels of atmospheric
gases and chemicals
present in the snow.

INVESTIGATING POLAR ICE
Glaciologists work in dug-out laboratories in the ice. The
polar ice sheet preserves snow fall from the past within its
layers. Compressed by more snow above, the layers get
thinner the more deeply they are buried (p. 59). Trapped
within the solid ice are bubbles of atmospheric gases and
traces of substances from the atmosphere. Therefore an ice
core may hold trapped volcanic dust from major volcanic
eruptions, nitric acid from the outer atmosphere, as well as
radioactive isotopes from nuclear testing.

The building blocks

OVER ONE HUNDRED CHEMICAL ELEMENTS combine to make up all matter. An element contains only one kind of atom, but atoms from different elements can join together to make a variety of substances called compounds. They do this by joining together (bonding) in different ways to make molecules. A few of the elements make up almost all of the types of naturally occurring compounds called minerals. These minerals make up rocks. Most rocks in the Earth's crust are composed of only eight of the chemical elements – oxygen, silicon, aluminium, iron, calcium, magnesium, sodium, and potassium. Two of these elements, silicon and oxygen, combine in silicates, which make up 75 per cent of the Earth's rocks. Most minerals are crystalline – the atoms that make up the crystals are arranged in an orderly fashion. It is the job of the mineralogist to understand what minerals are, where they are to be found, and what they can be used for.

GOLD IN NATURE
Gold is both an element and a mineral. It is found almost pure in nature where it may be in veins in rocks. The most pure natural gold is 99 per cent pure. For commercial purposes, it is often alloyed with silver. Gold forms cubic crystals and has a bright metallic lustre. It is very heavy, but not hard; it can be easily cut with a knife.

SILICON LOCKET
The chemical element silicon does not occur in nature. Silicon is always found as a silicate in combination with oxygen, and it takes a lot of chemical energy to separate out the silicon from the oxygen in a laboratory. When it was first separated, silicon was considered an exotic substance. This piece was mounted in a locket. Nowadays, silicon is made commercially for the electronics industry, where it is the raw material for the microchip.

New Mexico, USA

WHITE SANDS DESERT
This white sand is made of one mineral, gypsum, which has been weathered by wind (pp. 50-51). The composition of the mineral is calcium, in combination with sulphur and oxygen, to make the chemical calcium sulphate. The crystals of calcium sulphate in nature contain some water, and this combination goes to make up the mineral gypsum. Crystals of gypsum are soft and can be scratched with a fingernail. Gypsum forms crystals which are uncoloured and transparent, and sometimes white.

ELEMENTS IN THE EARTH'S CRUST
The crust, or lithosphere, is the outermost solid layer on the Earth's surface (pp. 6-7). Oxygen atoms are so large that almost all of the Earth's crust is made of them with the other elements just filling in the spaces between. Silicon atoms are small and fit happily between four oxygen atoms. Therefore the most abundant elements in the crust are those which readily combine with the relatively lightweight silicon and oxygen to make silicates. These elements fit into the physical spaces in the silicate framework and make up the common rock-forming minerals such as feldspars, pyroxenes, amphiboles, olivines, and micas.

DIFFERENT SILICATES
Two very different silicates are talc, familiar as the slippery white cosmetic powder, and beryl. Talc is a silicate of magnesium, crystallized with water in its structure. Beryl comes in various colours; the bright green variety in hard, clear crystals is the highly prized gemstone, emerald. Beryl is a silicate with aluminium in combination with the much rarer chemical element, beryllium.

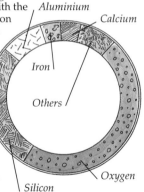

Aluminium

Calcium

Iron

Others

Silicon

Oxygen

Elements in the Earth's crust

SILICATES
Silicon and oxygen combine together to form the mineral quartz, and this commonly appears as sand. In silicates, the silicon atoms are each surrounded by four oxygen atoms, but the oxygen may be shared with neighbouring silicons. In this way the framework of silicates is made.

Si

O

O

O

O

Beryl

Talc

Telling minerals apart

Calcite, gypsum, and quartz look alike at first glance. All three may come as colourless, transparent crystals. All are used in industry in different ways, so it is important to be able to distinguish one from the other. Minerals are differentiated by their appearance, their colour, and whether they are transparent (an image can be read through them), translucent (let light through) or opaque (no light goes into the crystal). Other important properties are the hardness, the lustre, the streak (the colour of the powder they make), the density, and the crystal form and shape. In a laboratory more sophisticated tests may be done (p. 23).

Calcite

Gypsum

Quartz

WHICH MINERAL?
To determine the minerals in a piece of rock, a geologist would first look at the rock through a hand lens to check for crystal shape, texture, lustre, and colour. The next test would probably be the acid test.

1 ACID TEST
Dilute hydrochloric acid is dropped on to the area being tested. Carbonate rocks effervesce (fizz) to give off carbon dioxide gas when they meet acid. This identifies calcite.

Acid is dropped on to the rock

Calcite is a carbonate rock so it fizzes with acid

Rock containing calcite, gypsum, and quartz

2 HARDNESS TEST
The hardness of minerals is generally measured against a Mohs scale where talc is 1 (the softest), and diamond is 10, the hardest material known. A steel penknife is used here to do the test. Steel has a hardness of around 6, so quartz at a greater hardness, 7 on the Mohs scale, is not scratched by a knife, but calcite and gypsum are. Gypsum is softer than calcite so the penknife scratches it easily. Gypsum is so soft it can be scratched with a fingernail (hardness of 2).

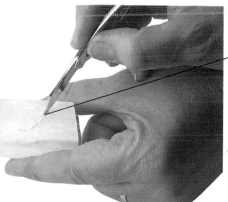

Steel penknife scratches the gypsum

Blue – low copper concentrations

Red – high copper concentrations

Yellow – no suitable data

3 FINDING QUARTZ
Another useful substance for hardness testing is window glass (5 on the Mohs scale). Calcite is softer than window glass (it has a hardness of only 3), so it will not scratch the glass. Neither will gypsum at 2 on the scale. Quartz is the only one of the three which scratches the glass. So the hardness tests confirm the findings on all three minerals.

Quartz scratches the window glass

COPPER CONCENTRATIONS IN SCOTLAND
The amount of various minerals in stream sediments is estimated by taking one sample every kilometre. The results are stored on a computer, and shown on a map. This map can show concentrations of copper and can be used for mineral exploration and for environmental reasons to check for contamination or pollution. Here high levels of copper are shown in dark red. The 60-million-year-old lavas of the Inner Hebrides Islands are high in copper, and so are granite regions in the Highlands. Copper also shows up high in industrial areas, where there is no relationship to the underlying rocks; the concentration is the direct result of human activity.

Investigating rocks

THE FIRST SYSTEMATIC BOOK ON MINERALOGY was written by Agricola (p. 8), in the 16th century. Written in Latin, it was called *De Natura Fossilium*. The word "fossil" then meant "things dug up", and included chiefly minerals and rocks. Agricola based his writings on his own observations, rather than using the speculative or hopeful reasoning that had characterized the writings of the ancient Greeks, and, later, the alchemists. In the 18th century the Age of Enlightenment encouraged many thinkers to contemplate the origin of the Earth and of rocks. A controversy raged between the Neptunists, led by Abraham Werner, and the Plutonists, who believed the origin of some rocks was undoubtedly volcanic, led by James Hutton (p. 8). Europe's scientists were divided into two camps. Towards the end of the 18th century travel became easier, allowing scientists to observe directly many different types of rocks in different places. In 1830 Charles Lyell (p. 62) published his influential work, *Principles of Geology*. This book influenced other geologists who responded to Lyell's theories about the slow, gradual nature of the Earth's processes.

Neptune – the Roman god of the sea

JAMES DANA
James Dana (1813-1895) was an American geologist best known for his *System of Mineralogy* (1837). He suggested that landscapes were shaped by the ongoing forces of weathering and erosion. His predecessors had imagined that sudden catastrophic events, such as earthquakes, were responsible.

ROCKS FROM WATER
Abraham Werner (1750-1817) was a German geologist who put forward the ideas of Neptunism. The Neptunists opposed the Plutonists (p. 8). Neptunists believed that the chemicals that made up rocks had been dissolved in the ocean waters, and all rocks including basalt had come out of this solution. Werner's fame spread from the eloquence of his personal teachings and the dedicated work of his students.

Geologists in the field

Geologists fall into many categories such as palaeontologists, petrologists, and geochemists, but they all study the Earth, and the place to start is in the rocks. In the field, geologists record their observations in notebooks, take photographs, and collect specimens. The specimens are labelled and wrapped for transport back to the laboratory.

Geological hammer

Abraham Werner

Hand lens

TOOLS OF THE TRADE
A geologist uses a hammer to break off rock samples fresh from the solid bedrock. This ensures that the samples collected have truly come from the solid rocks of the place being mapped. The small hammer is used for trimming rock samples. A chisel helps in splitting rocks. The hand lens is used to look in detail at the texture of rock, and to see if any fossils are present.

Trimming hammer

Chisel

Chisel

SMITH'S MAP (1819)
The first geological maps were published at the beginning of the 19th century. Geological maps show relief features such as mountains or roads, as well as the different rocks that appear at the surface, and use different colours to show their different ages. William Smith (p. 26) published the first geological map of Britain in 1815.

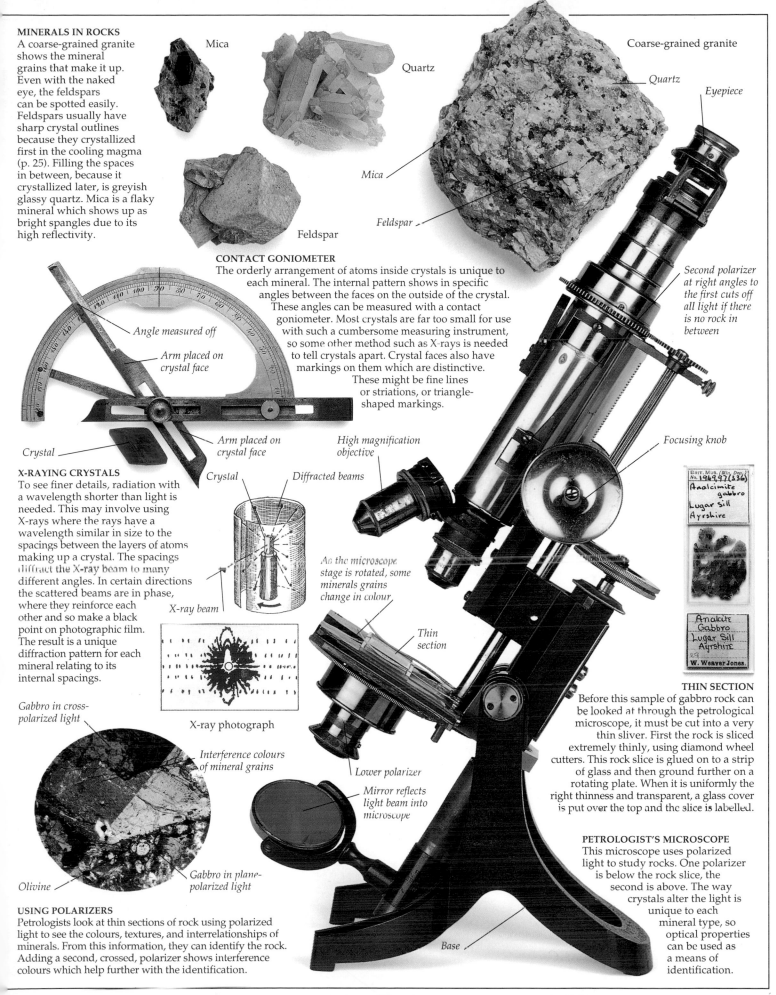

MINERALS IN ROCKS

A coarse-grained granite shows the mineral grains that make it up. Even with the naked eye, the feldspars can be spotted easily. Feldspars usually have sharp crystal outlines because they crystallized first in the cooling magma (p. 25). Filling the spaces in between, because it crystallized later, is greyish glassy quartz. Mica is a flaky mineral which shows up as bright spangles due to its high reflectivity.

Mica

Quartz

Feldspar

Coarse-grained granite

Quartz

Mica

Feldspar

Eyepiece

Second polarizer at right angles to the first cuts off all light if there is no rock in between

CONTACT GONIOMETER

The orderly arrangement of atoms inside crystals is unique to each mineral. The internal pattern shows in specific angles between the faces on the outside of the crystal. These angles can be measured with a contact goniometer. Most crystals are far too small for use with such a cumbersome measuring instrument, so some other method such as X-rays is needed to tell crystals apart. Crystal faces also have markings on them which are distinctive. These might be fine lines or striations, or triangle-shaped markings.

Angle measured off

Arm placed on crystal face

Crystal

Arm placed on crystal face

High magnification objective

Focusing knob

X-RAYING CRYSTALS

To see finer details, radiation with a wavelength shorter than light is needed. This may involve using X-rays where the rays have a wavelength similar in size to the spacings between the layers of atoms making up a crystal. The spacings diffract the X-ray beam to many different angles. In certain directions the scattered beams are in phase, where they reinforce each other and so make a black point on photographic film. The result is a unique diffraction pattern for each mineral relating to its internal spacings.

Crystal

Diffracted beams

X-ray beam

As the microscope stage is rotated, some minerals grains change in colour

Thin section

Gabbro in cross-polarized light

X-ray photograph

Interference colours of mineral grains

Olivine

Gabbro in plane-polarized light

Lower polarizer

Mirror reflects light beam into microscope

Base

BRIT. MUS. (Min. Dep.)
No. 1949.97 (336)
Analcimite gabbro
Lugar Sill
Ayrshire

Analcite
Gabbro
Lugar Sill
Ayrshire
W. Weaver Jones.

THIN SECTION

Before this sample of gabbro rock can be looked at through the petrological microscope, it must be cut into a very thin sliver. First the rock is sliced extremely thinly, using diamond wheel cutters. This rock slice is glued on to a strip of glass and then ground further on a rotating plate. When it is uniformly the right thinness and transparent, a glass cover is put over the top and the slice is labelled.

USING POLARIZERS

Petrologists look at thin sections of rock using polarized light to see the colours, textures, and interrelationships of minerals. From this information, they can identify the rock. Adding a second, crossed, polarizer shows interference colours which help further with the identification.

PETROLOGIST'S MICROSCOPE

This microscope uses polarized light to study rocks. One polarizer is below the rock slice, the second is above. The way crystals alter the light is unique to each mineral type, so optical properties can be used as a means of identification.

Igneous rocks

Guy Tancrède de Dolomieu (1750-1801)

IGNEOUS ROCKS ARE THE PRIMARY, original material that makes up the Earth's surface. The first rocks on the Earth were igneous rocks; they formed as the planet started to cool. Magma is the name of the molten material that solidifies and crystallizes in a complex way to make the range of different minerals found in igneous rocks. It is continually being produced deep inside the Earth. This process cannot be observed so scientists must guess at the mechanism. Because Vesuvius continued to display some volcanic activity throughout the 18th century, French mineralogist Dolomieu was able to watch an active volcano. He became convinced that the origin of the lava was deep inside the Earth. Some magma cools and solidifies inside the Earth's crust in a mass known as an igneous intrusion (p. 51). At the beginning of the 20th century, Norman Bowen (1887-1956), a Canadian petrologist, studied the way silicate liquids crystallized as they cooled, working with silicate melts which were an approximation to natural magma. He discovered that metal oxide minerals crystallized out first, as they had the highest melting points. The later crystals that formed were a product of interaction between the early crystals and the liquid that remained, which had a different chemical composition.

Weather carries loose grains which collect to make sedimentary rock

If rocks are heated enough they may melt to become new magma

Sedimentary rocks become buried

Sedimentary rocks may be heated and compressed into metamorphic rocks

WEARING DOWN A MOUNTAIN RANGE
When a mountain range is made, the deep-down rocks are elevated (pp. 46-47). As the mountain range grows higher, so the mountain tops are worn away by the weather over millions of years. This granite on Dartmoor in England crystallized many kilometres down in the Earth's crust and was part of an igneous intrusion known as a batholith (p. 51). Erosion has worn away a whole mountain range leaving the hilltop granite tor, the word originally coming from the Celtic name for granite summits in this part of the world.

Haytor, Dartmoor, southern Britain

Eroded granite

THE ROCK CYCLE
The rock cycle continually renews the surface of the Earth. When igneous rocks meet the Earth's atmosphere, they are changed. New minerals are formed, and the crystal grains are prised apart and carried away by the weather to form sediments. They become sedimentary rock (pp. 26-27) and can then be heated or compressed into metamorphic rock (pp. 28-29), and even melted to make new igneous rock.

Orthorhombic crystals

Monoclinic crystals

Powdered sulphur crystals

Melted sulphur

LARGE CRYSTALS
When a liquid cools slowly, it makes large crystals because there is time for the atoms to find their place in the orderly crystal arrangement. The element sulphur makes orthorhombic or monoclinic crystals depending on the temperature at which the crystals grow. The granite of Haytor cooled over maybe 1 million years so the crystals are as large as 5 cm (2 in) across.

HEATING CRYSTALS
Powdered crystals of sulphur can be heated until they melt. If the conditions of cooling are faster, needle-like monoclinic crystals form at about 90°C (194°F). These crystals grow in nature in the heat of a volcanic fumarole, or hot spring. They form around the mouth of the fumarole where the cooling occurs.

Rapid cooling

Plastic-like sulphur

CHILLED CRYSTALS
A liquid which is chilled suddenly may freeze to a glassy structure which lacks the orderly internal arrangement of crystals. The glassy structure may look quite different from the equivalent crystalline material. Chilled sulphur is stretchy and plastic. A silicate melt or magma which is chilled rapidly makes a natural glass. Over millions of years the glass may begin to turn to crystals.

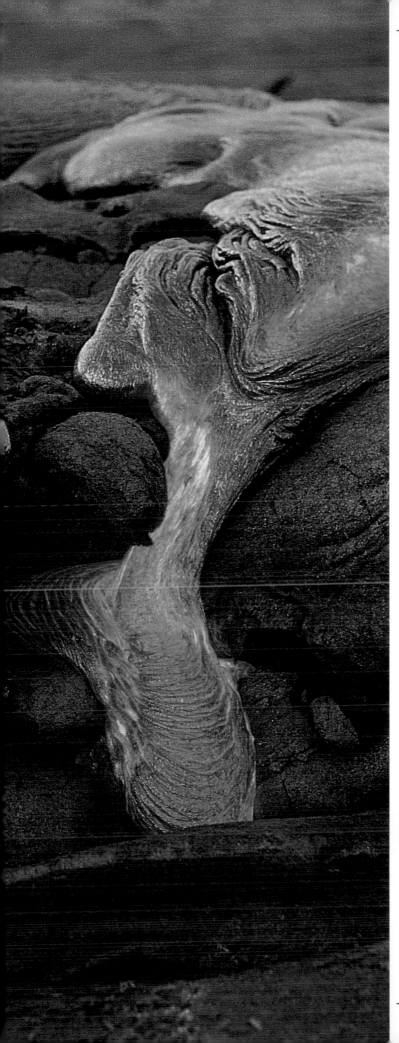

THE RECYCLING OF MAGMA

Magma originates in the Earth's mantle. Sometimes a little melting takes place in the mantle and if the drops of melt join up they start to migrate towards the Earth's surface. Basalt is the igneous rock nearest in composition to its parent material, the mantle. Basalt-like rocks erupt as lava flows (like those on Hawaii, left) to make up the ocean floor. When ocean floor goes back into the mantle, part of the basaltic rock is melted. This new magma makes its way back towards the Earth's surface, changing in composition as it travels and it becomes granite.

Volcano *Continental crust*

Ocean floor slides back into mantle *Rising magma*

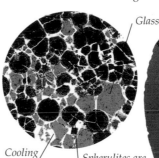

Glass

Cooling cracks *Spherulites are beginnings of crystals*

Thin section of obsidian under cross-polarized light

OBSIDIAN

Obsidian is a natural glass made from magma which was cooled too quickly to crystallize. When it erupts as lava, there is no opportunity for the atoms to arrange themselves in an orderly fashion.

Large crystals against a fine-grained background mass is called porphyritic texture

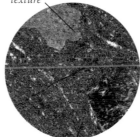

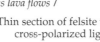

Crystal cooled as lava flows

Thin section of felsite under cross-polarized light

FELSITE

Felsite's larger crystals of quartz and feldspar grew during slow cooling (before eruption), while the small crystals result from rapid cooling at eruption.

Quartz formed later *Mica fits into spaces*

Feldspar crystallized first

Thin section of granite under cross-polarized light

GRANITE

Granite cools most slowly of these three rocks. Obsidian, felsite, and granite are formed from magma of about the same chemical composition – the difference is solely due to the rate at which they cooled.

Sedimentary rocks

ROCKS THAT COME INTO CONTACT with the atmosphere and with water are gradually weathered (pp. 50-51), even the hard lavas and granite. Water seeps in between the mineral grains and chemically reacts with the rock to break it down. Particles of the weathered rock are removed by falling rain, or are blown away by the wind and dropped elsewhere. In the new location, layers of sediment are formed, which may become buried by more and more layers. These layers may also contain organic material such as plants and the remains of dead creatures. Eventually the sediments harden and become compacted. Ground water percolates through the sediment, leaving behind minerals which cement the sediment grains together. In this way the sediment is lithified (becomes rock). By understanding how modern sediment forms, it is possible to reconstruct the environment of times gone by – the palaeoenvironment – and to make palaeogeographic maps showing the geography of land masses that existed many millions of years ago.

WILLIAM SMITH (1769-1839)
Smith was an English engineer who surveyed routes for canals. He recognized the same types of rock in different places and realized that individual layers of sedimentary rocks were characterized by similar groupings of fossils. He concluded that the oldest rocks were in the lowest layer.

QUARRY OF SAND
The layers of sand in this English quarry are around 100 million years old and were laid in a shallow sea just below the wave depth. The layers of sandstone are overlaid by a layer of grey-coloured boulder clay (p. 59). The sand is quarried as sports turf sand for golf courses and pitches, and for filtering drinking water.

SANDSTONE
This sandstone is made from grains of sand, like modern desert sand (p. 55). The grains are visible even without a magnifying glass. A specimen of sandstone may also show changes of colour and banding. The layers of the original sands may be the result of the desert wind sorting the sand grains into different sizes or densities. Some sandstones show mineral grains in coloured bands. These minerals, heavier than ordinary sand grains, are sometimes concentrated in layers.

Grain of quartz

Thin section of sandstone in cross-polarized light

Red sandstone

Even texture

Pebble

HOW SEDIMENT IS MADE
Fragments of older rocks make up sediment. During a flood, heavy rain loosens the weathered sand and gravel from mountain slopes. Along with the soil (pp. 52-53), this loosened sediment is carried away in flood waters and is dropped when and where the water current slows. A river in flood always has coloured turbid water from the sediment it carries, which could be a mixture of mud, sand, and pebbles (p. 57).

Fossil shell

Origins of oil

Oil is derived from the remains of dead plants. They decay and sink to the seabed, where they become entombed in the thickening sediment. The temperature increases as the sediments are buried ever deeper, and oily liquids are boiled off from the organic remains. The oily material travels through the pores of permeable rocks (p. 15) and seeps into sandstone or limestone. Here the oil collects in the pore spaces in the rock.

Shelly limestone

Natural oil

Sandstone borehole core

LIMESTONE
Plants and animals which live in sea or river water use calcium bicarbonate in solution in the water to make calcium carbonate. Animals may use this to construct shells or skeletons, while plants become surrounded with limy mud. Eventually the mud becomes limestone which often contains the shells of the creatures that made the calcium carbonate.

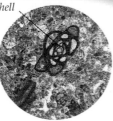

Fossil shell

Thin section of limestone in plane-polarized light

MUDSTONE
It is impossible to see the grains that make up mudstone without a high-powered microscope. The minute flakes of clay and silt are the smallest particles of sediment to come from the weathering of older rocks. Clay is derived from weathering of feldspars. Grains of silt, which might be quartz or feldspar, are slightly larger in size. Mudstone forms in river estuaries, lakes, and in the sea.

CONGLOMERATE
Sediment that contains many rounded pebbles, usually with some sand filling in the spaces between, is called conglomerate. Originally the sediment may have been gravel in a river bed, the pebbles having been carried along during a flood and dumped along with sand.

Pebbles are made of the hard mineral quartz

OIL-BEARING ROCK
When sediment becomes rock, there are almost always spaces between the individual grains of sediment which are not filled with cementing minerals. In the pore spaces of this sandstone rock, 1.5 litres (3 pints) of oil were trapped under pressure. However, it is not possible to extract all oil from rock. Because of the surface tension and the viscosity of oil, some oil remains clinging to the rock grains.

Pipeline   *Drilling rig*

Impermeable rock

DRILLING FOR OIL
If a rock structure is suitable, oil sometimes collects. If it is trapped in the rock layers, it can be collected for commercial use. Potential oil-bearing structures may be detected from the Earth's surface or the seabed. The geologist plays a vital role in predicting where oil traps might exist.

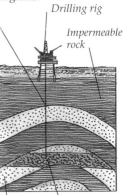

Permeable rock   *Trapped oil*

Shell

Sand

Metamorphic rocks

METAMORPHIC ROCKS ARE ROCKS that have been changed. Previously, they were igneous, sedimentary, or other metamorphic rocks. Almost all metamorphism happens deep in young mountain ranges as rocks are folded and compressed underneath other rocks. Although rock never actually melts, the texture and nature of the rock may become like new, made of different, metamorphic crystals (p. 23), with no sign of the original minerals or textures. Part of this occurs in response to pressure, and part is the result of the heat. Metamorphism takes a long time, first for the rock to be buried to a depth where metamorphism can begin, and then for the solid recrystallization to take place. Eventually, metamorphic rocks are exposed at the Earth's surface, but only after the mountain chain is uplifted and eroded deeply (pp. 46-47). This process in which sediment is buried and made into metamorphic rocks may take 100 million years.

THE EXPERIMENTER
Sir James Hall (1761-1832) was a Scottish baronet who took powdered limestone and sealed it in a gun barrel to maintain the pressure, then heated it in his foundry. The material that emerged was a crystalline marble. He had metamorphosed the sedimentary rock.

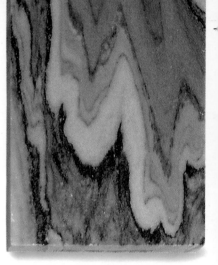

STREAKED CIPOLLINO MARBLE
Limestone made of pure calcium carbonate (p. 27) recrystallizes during metamorphism to a pure white marble. Many limestones contain quartz sand, or some clay, or iron. When these are metamorphosed, the result is coloured marble, often with folded banding. Many metamorphic rocks show evidence of folding or fracturing, indicating that they reacted as though they were either plastic or brittle (p. 20) during mountain building.

CONTACT WITH HOT GRANITE
When molten granite intrudes into rocks in mountain ranges, the rocks are metamorphosed around the granite. The halo of changed rock is called a metamorphic aureole. New minerals grow in response to high temperatures, for example, limestone becomes marble.

Sandstone

Metamorphic aureole

Limestone

Granite

Marble

INCREASING THE PRESSURE
Metamorphism can transform a featureless mudstone into a sparkling crystalline rock. Muds laid down in shallow seas are carried down during mountain building to deeper levels. The first sign of metamorphism is growth of microscopic crystals of mica. Pressure may cause these to be aligned, which produces slate (1). Phyllite (2) has been recrystallized more intensely, so that the mica crystals are larger and can be seen as a shimmer on the rock surface. Even deeper or longer burial in the mountain range creates a schist which may have large mica crystals, and grains or crystals of kyanite (3), whose crystallization is also helped by heat.

Increase in pressure

1. Slate

2. Phyllite

SPLITTING SLATE FOR ROOFS
Mica crystals in slate are all parallel to each other. The slate splitter knows the direction, and splits or cleaves the slate along it. This is called the cleavage direction.

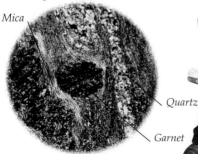

Mica

Quartz

Garnet

MUDSTONE MAKES GARNET
In mudstone, the first metamorphic minerals to grow are mica crystals, orientating themselves in the direction of least pressure. The garnet grew later, pushing mica crystals out of the way.

Blue kyanite

3. Kyanite schist

SOLID-STATE RECRYSTALLIZATION

All the recrystallization that is part of metamorphism happens in the solid state. It is similar to the recrystallization that happens when metal is heated and beaten to make wrought iron. The original metal is made of crystals which, after heating in the furnace, adjust their structure in response to the pressure applied by beating. At the points where crystals meet, individual atoms move away to a place where pressure is lower. There they align themselves with the crystal structure and add on to it.

1. Chiastolite hornfels

Chiastolite crystal

Garnet

Increase in heat and pressure

2. Garnet hornfels

Mica-rich area

3. Migmatite

Quartz-rich area

Steel rod

Changed crystal structure

Rod heated to red heat in a furnace

Rod reaches white heat

The shape changes without melting

Thin section of titanium

ROLLED METAL

The texture of this titanium metal has been altered by cold rolling. Crystals near the surface have responded to the pressure put on them and have adjusted their structure to fit in with it. In the same way, but with heating as well, rocks metamorphose without melting. Under some circumstances, melting may take place in mountain ranges, making a new magma. This can happen if very hot granite magmas ascend in an active mountain range and cause melting of the surrounding rocks, increasing the volume of the granite magma.

New crystals grow in the rod

HEAT AND PRESSURE

Mudstone or shale can grow crystals of the mineral chiastolite (1) when it is in contact with a magma. The resulting hard rock is called hornfels. More intense metamorphism, at greater depth and temperature, may grow garnet crystals (2) instead. Intense metamorphism, where rock is heated almost to melting, produces migmatite, or mixed rock (3).

Rod is beaten with hammer

Intricate shapes may be made from the beating process

Mica-rich layers weather more easily

RED HOT METAL

A plain steel rod can be fashioned into intricate patterns by heating and beating it. The smith who works the metal is making the crystals reorientate themselves as they grow in certain directions.

REGIONAL METAMORPHISM

This gneiss in northern France was part of a mountain range which was eroded down to a plain long before the Alps were formed. Gneiss is a rock formed through metamorphism of whole regions. Such regional metamorphism happens during the birth of a mountain range.

The challenge of the ocean

THE BEGINNINGS OF MODERN OCEANOGRAPHY lie at the end of the 19th century with oceanic surveys such as that conducted by the British research vessel *Challenger*. The USA was proposing to explore the Atlantic and Pacific oceans, with Alexandre Agassiz (1835–1910) as joint leader, and German and Swedish ships, too, were venturing into the Atlantic. The British government was persuaded to support the *Challenger* expedition to uphold Britain's international prestige. It was hoped that *Challenger*'s exploration would be able to answer pressing questions of the day. Was the deep ocean populated with living creatures? Could ocean currents be measured to confirm theories about how oceanic waters circulated? If sediment lay on the ocean floor, would it be the familiar chalk? *Challenger* was able to answer some of these questions, but the oceanic circulation remained a controversy even at the end of the voyage. It is now known that many variable factors influence the currents. By taking depth soundings, *Challenger* did discover submarine mountains in the middle of the Atlantic Ocean (pp. 38-39), and found the Mariana Trench, 11,033 m (36,000 ft) down in the Pacific Ocean.

IMAGINING THE DEEP
In 1869 French writer Jules Verne (1828-1905) wrote the novel *Twenty Thousand Leagues under the Sea*. It tells of a submarine whose technology was advanced far beyond its time. In the 20th century the technology of Verne's submarine is commonplace. To appreciate Verne's far-sightedness, the reader must imagine back to the time when this was science fiction, written about an uncharted region of the Earth.

Reading taken on stem

Glass flask

THE HYDROMETER
Oceanic water was sampled by *Challenger* to discover how salinity and temperature vary with depth and location. This hydrometer measured salinity. The warm surface current in the Atlantic Ocean – the Gulf Stream – was already known, mapped by Benjamin Franklin in the 18th century. *Challenger* showed that there was much colder water at deeper levels which could be the compensating current of cold water.

HISTORIC VOYAGE
The *Challenger*'s epic voyage lasted from 1872 to 1875. The ship sailed 111,000 km (59,900 nautical miles), measuring the ocean and collecting samples. The expedition did not include a physicist. If it had, maybe the profusion of *Challenger*'s observations could have been used to work out the inter-relationships between salinity, temperature and water density, ocean bottom slope, winds, and the effects of evaporation and rainfall, which together affect oceanic circulation.

Engraving showing a hydrometer suspended in liquid

Mercury acts as a weight

END OF THE FLAT EARTH THEORY
In the 16th century an expedition led by the Portuguese Ferdinand Magellan (1480-1521) sailed around the world, finally proving that it was not flat. Magellan tried to calculate the depth of the ocean as he sailed. However, navigators usually kept in sight of land. Here the water is shallower than the great ocean deeps, and the bottom sediments are derived from the land.

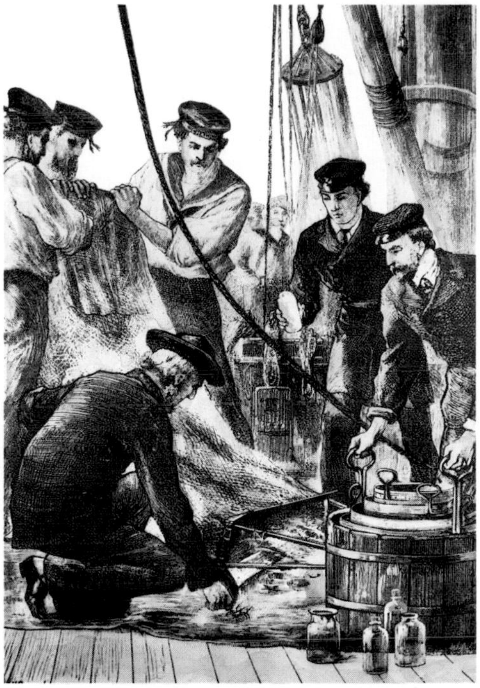

Sifting through dredged sediment on *Challenger*

ON BOARD SHIP
The naturalists on *Challenger* charted ocean-bottom sediments and their relationship to life in the sea. Dredges were used to sample these sediments. The samples showed that the plankton *Globigerina* lived in the surface water of almost all parts of the ocean. Investigations showed that when *Globigerina* dies, the shells sink to the seabed and make the fine carbonate mud known as Globigerina ooze (p. 13).

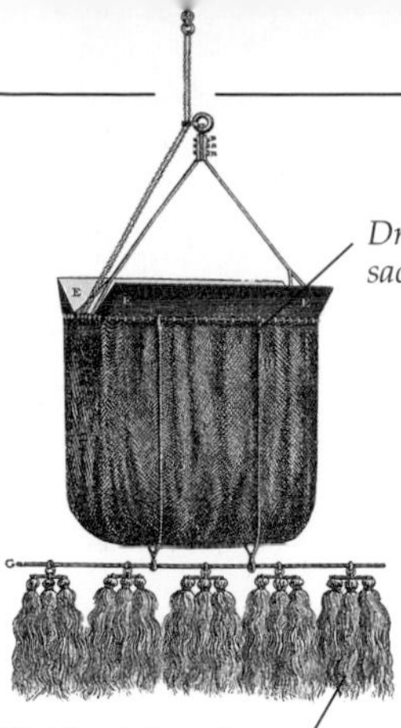

Dredge sack
Flat-headed swabs drag the net along the sea floor

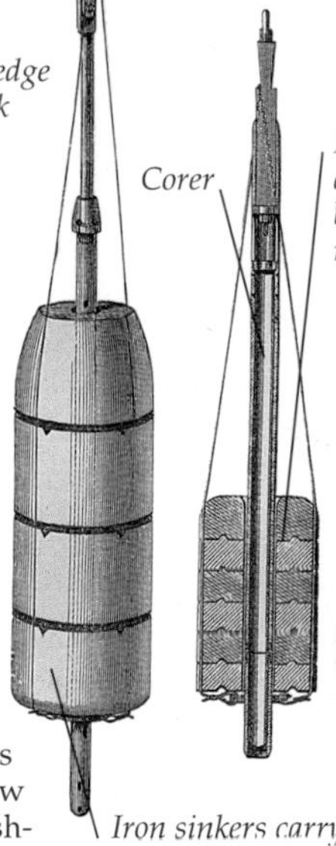

Corer
Iron sinkers detach before resurfacing
Iron sinkers carry line down and force the corer into the sludge

DREDGING THE DEPTHS
Dredges and cores (p. 13) were used to collect material from all parts of the seabed. Although water samples showed that *Globigerina* lived in the sunlit shallow waters of the Atlantic, the dredges brought up reddish-coloured clay from the deep ocean floor instead of the ooze. The deeper the water, the less sign there was of any *Globigerina* shells at the ocean bed. The *Challenger* team supposed, rightly, that at such huge depths *Globigerina* shells had dissolved in sea water; the red clay was dust blown from the land.

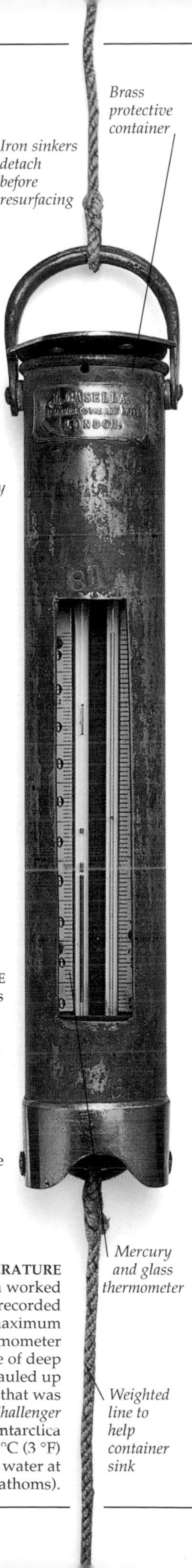

Brass protective container
LONDON.
Mercury and glass thermometer
Weighted line to help container sink

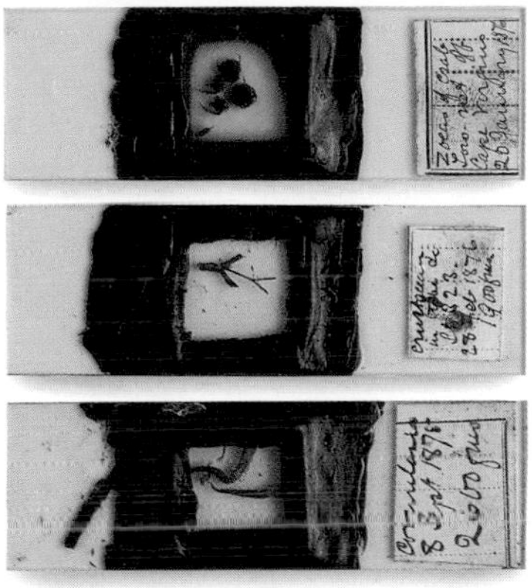

Slides containing samples

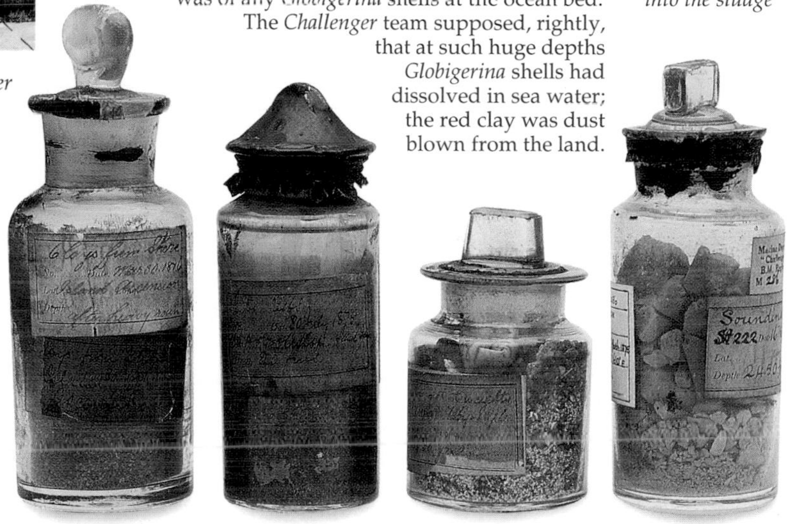

Clay from seashore — Globigerina ooze — Shelly sand — Sediment

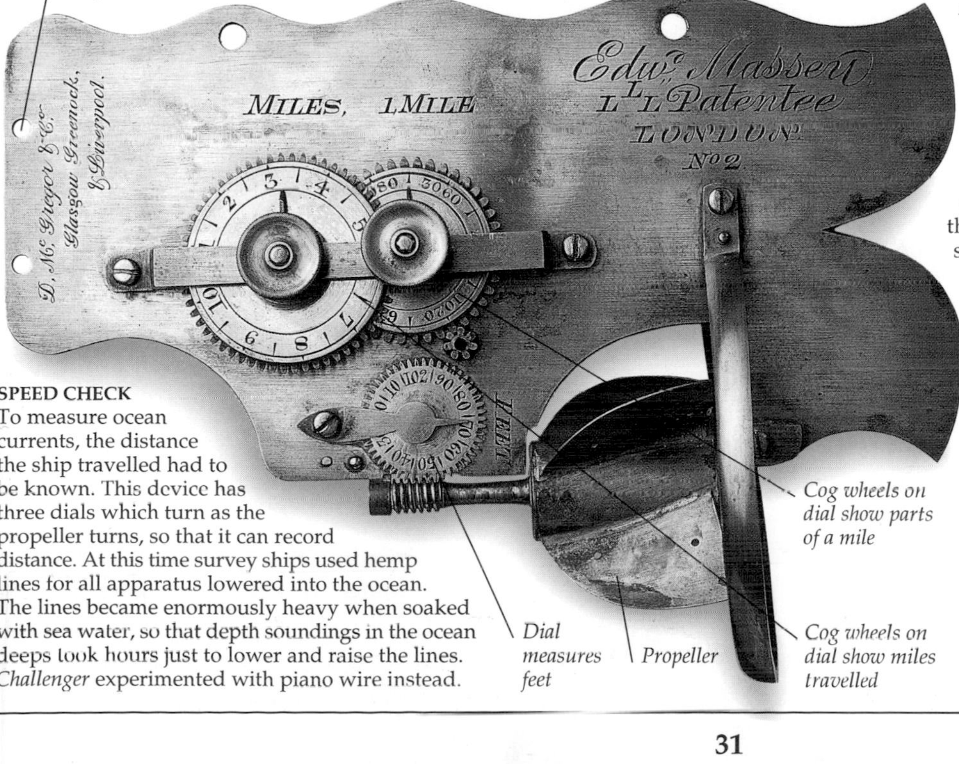

Hemp line attached here
MILES, 1 MILE
L L Patentee
LONDON
No 2
FEET
Cog wheels on dial show parts of a mile
Dial measures feet
Propeller
Cog wheels on dial show miles travelled

ASSEMBLING THE EVIDENCE
The task of sending samples to scientists for study and storage, and of writing up and publishing the results of *Challenger*'s work took 15 years. The material was bottled up with labels that gave latitude and longitude, the depth of water where the sample was collected, and the type of material (ooze or clay, for example).

SPEED CHECK
To measure ocean currents, the distance the ship travelled had to be known. This device has three dials which turn as the propeller turns, so that it can record distance. At this time survey ships used hemp lines for all apparatus lowered into the ocean. The lines became enormously heavy when soaked with sea water, so that depth soundings in the ocean deeps took hours just to lower and raise the lines. *Challenger* experimented with piano wire instead.

TAKING THE TEMPERATURE
At first the *Challenger* team worked with thermometers which recorded only minimum and maximum temperatures. This thermometer registered the temperature of deep water even when it was hauled up to the ship through water that was either cooler or warmer. *Challenger* discovered that off Antarctica surface water was –16 °C (3 °F) colder than water at 550 m (300 fathoms).

Modern oceanography

LIFE IN THE OCEAN DEPTHS
The deep ocean is a dark place. Knowing the amount of light in ocean water is vital to our understanding of where and how oceanic plants and animals live. Photosynthesis can take place at light levels as low as 1 per cent of sunlight. Creatures like the angler fish, which emit light to lure their prey, add significantly to light levels in the dark parts of the ocean.

Twentieth-century oceanographic surveys have revolutionized our view of the planet and how it works by revealing the surface features – the topography – and nature of the ocean floor. In the early 1960s there was a plan to drill a borehole to penetrate the mantle. The "Mohole" was to be drilled where the crust was thinnest. This meant drilling in deep water from a floating ship. Seismic investigation (p. 40) had already shown that the ocean floor has a layered structure. The Mohole would sample the ocean floor and reveal the nature of the layers. Mohole never reached the Moho – the boundary where the mantle meets the crust (p. 40). Instead, in 1964, the US drilling ship *Glomar Challenger* began to roam the oceans, drilling into sediment and ocean floor. Detailed mapping is now carried out by remote sensing apparatus towed from floating ships, and in orbiting satellites. Computers are used to visualize oceanic water circulation.

INVESTIGATING THE DEEP
Glomar Challenger's samples led to an understanding of sea-floor spreading (pp. 38-39). They revealed that nearest to the submarine mountains (p. 30) the basalt is young, and further away it is older. Not only that, but near these ridges the oldest sediments on the hard basaltic floor are present-day sediments. Further from the ridge, these present-day sediments lay over progressively older sediments.

PLANKTON NETS
The food chain in the oceans begins with the inorganic nutrients carried in oceanic currents. The smallest plants and animals are plankton, which float passively. They range from microscopic algae to shrimps. The larger ocean life feeds on this plankton. Oceanographers use special plankton nets to assess the amounts of plankton, and to discover the relative proportions of plant and animal plankton in a given area. Sampling in the seas around Antarctica showed that in oceanic water the animal plankton grazed on the plant plankton, but in coastal waters they fed on bacteria.

PLANKTON FROM SATELLITE
Modern oceanographers and marine geologists use sophisticated technology in their work. Satellites can map the distribution of plankton in surface water – here in the Indian and Pacific oceans. Satellite imagery can also help to spot changes in temperature and salinity in oceanic waters which, though small, may have profound effects on oceanic currents.

Yellow shows average plankton density

Red shows the highest density of plankton

Pink shows the lowest density of plankton

Blue shows a low plankton density

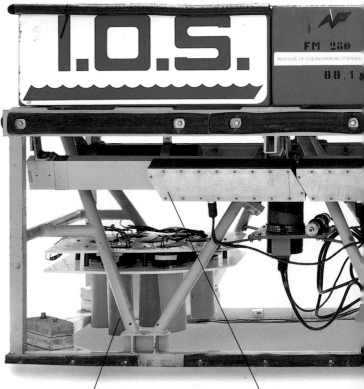

Sub-bottom profiler provides information about underlying sediments

Sonar instrument mounted on the side

Sonar imaging

In ocean water, below a few hundred metres, it is too dark for light imaging to tell us anything about the ocean floor. Sound waves, however, can be used instead. Echo sounding was the first such method. Modern sophisticated sound imaging with computer enhancement can now give detailed pictures, and make maps of areas of special interest, such as the economic exclusion zones off coastlines.

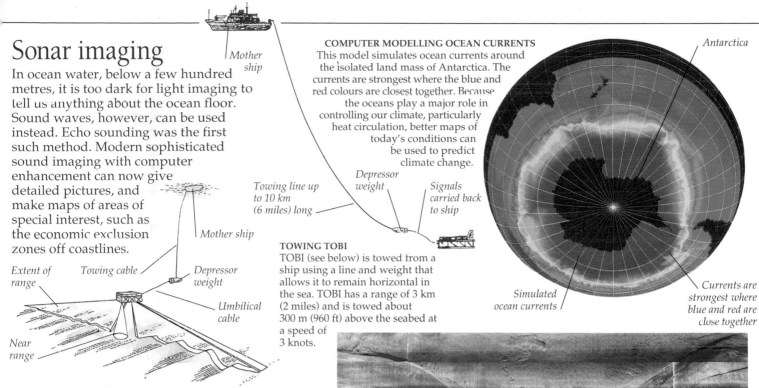

Mother ship

Towing line up to 10 km (6 miles) long

Depressor weight

Signals carried back to ship

Extent of range

Towing cable

Mother ship

Depressor weight

Umbilical cable

Near range

COMPUTER MODELLING OCEAN CURRENTS
This model simulates ocean currents around the isolated land mass of Antarctica. The currents are strongest where the blue and red colours are closest together. Because the oceans play a major role in controlling our climate, particularly heat circulation, better maps of today's conditions can be used to predict climate change.

Antarctica

Simulated ocean currents

Currents are strongest where blue and red are close together

TOWING TOBI
TOBI (see below) is towed from a ship using a line and weight that allows it to remain horizontal in the sea. TOBI has a range of 3 km (2 miles) and is towed about 300 m (960 ft) above the seabed at a speed of 3 knots.

HOW SONAR WORKS
Acoustic images of the ocean floor can be produced by a scanner that transmits regular sound pulses. The echoes show up on a display. The units which make up the image (pixels) cover an area the size of a snooker table. Future developments may include a scatterometer to determine the character of the sediment while fibre-optic towing cables will bring the possibility of remote-videoing.

TOWED OCEAN BOTTOM INSTRUMENT (TOBI)
TOBI is a remote-controlled vehicle which is towed behind a ship in water up to 6000 m (20,000 ft) deep. It acts as a platform for a variety of oceanographic instruments. Its sensors send data through the umbilical cable to the ship where they are stored on optical disc. The sound pictures, called sonographs, can image by sonar an object as small as 2 m (6 ft) across.

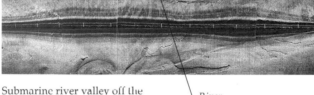

Submarine river valley off the west coast of the USA

River channel

SUBMARINE RIVER
This TOBI image shows a submarine river valley scoured by flowing sediments. The sediment would normally sit on the continental shelf but it has been disturbed and has flowed down the shelf to the ocean floor.

SHORE

EUROSHORE

6 000 m   FM 280 9005-1   6 000 m

46,1 Kp   88,1 Kg   46,1 Kp

I.O.S.

Foam buoyancy

Electronic housing

Umbilical cable

Sensors at various locations

Electronic components housed here

Open aluminium frame

Continental drift

Atlas holding the world on his shoulders

The shapes and sizes of the continents are continually changing, though extremely slowly. The earliest maps of the south Atlantic Ocean showed a remarkable fit between the shapes of the coastlines on either side. It took time to understand what kind of mechanism could move the continents to make this happen (pp. 36-37). It is now known that the continents are moving, and the rate – only a few centimetres a year – can be measured. In 1915 Alfred Wegener (1880-1930) published his theory of drifting continents. This told of an ancient "supercontinent" that scientists called Pangaea. When Pangaea started to break up some 300 million years ago (abbreviated to 300 Ma), the Atlantic Ocean began to grow in the place where Africa split away from South America. Eduard Suess (p. 42) proposed that the southern continent be called Gondwanaland, after a region inhabited by the Gonds in India. Slightly later, the northern continent Laurasia was split apart to separate North America from Europe, isolating Greenland. It seems that the Earth's processes continually either split supercontinents apart or move continents together to make supercontinents, in cyclic events that take hundreds of millions of years to complete.

SIR FRANCIS BACON (1561-1626)
Following the discovery of America, and the mapping of the coastlines of the Atlantic Ocean, the English philosopher Francis Bacon suggested that the coastlines of the two continents seemed to fit each other as though they had been torn apart.

MAPPING THE WORLD
In 1569 Flemish cartographer Gerhardus Mercator (1512-1594) produced a world map based on knowledge brought back by the navigators of the time. Coastlines were becoming better known from exploration of the Americas and the Pacific Ocean. The journeys of Magellan, Vasco de Gama, and Columbus had, in a short period, doubled the known area of the Earth. Mercator's map showed that the land areas are only a small part of the surface of the Earth, with the ocean regions covering three-quarters of the map. Ancient ideas about the ocean, its depth, and its surface extent were previously vague.

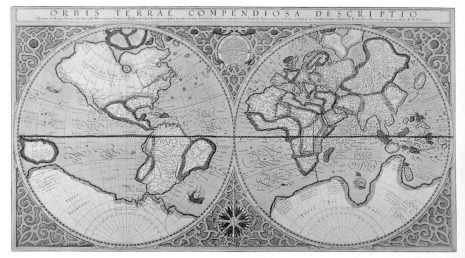

The skull of *Lystrosaurus*

LYSTROSAURUS
Fossil remains of land-living animals such as *Lystrosaurus* show that the southern continents were once linked together. The same types of fossils are found in all the southern continents; the animals must have roamed freely over lands now separated by ocean.

Namibian coastline

NAMIBIAN DESERT
Rocks found in Namibia in western Africa are similar to those in Brazil in South America. They were formed long before the break up of the southern continent Gondwanaland.

PANGAEA

Wegener's maps of the drifting continents placed them all together in Late Carboniferous times as the great supercontinent which he called Pangaea, a Greek name for "all the Earth". In the Eocene period, Greenland still connected Europe and North America. Geologists were divided in their acceptance of Wegener's elegant idea mainly because geophysicists could not suggest a mechanism for how the continents moved.

Pangaea in the Late Carboniferous

Shallow seas

Laurasia

Pangaea in the Eocene

Gondwanaland

Common snail

SUPPORTING EVIDENCE

Formidable data supported Wegener's theory. The distributions of plants and land animals in North America and western Europe were shown to have many similarities. The garden snail, found in southern Germany and the British Isles, was also found in the eastern USA.

GONDWANALAND DRIFTING

Wegener drew the southern continents close to the South Pole because Carboniferous rocks showed that part of Gondwanaland was covered with an ice sheet. Matching lavas 200 million years old are found in both Africa and South America. These may have been part of the Earth's internal stability that started the break up of Gondwanaland.

Alfred Wegener

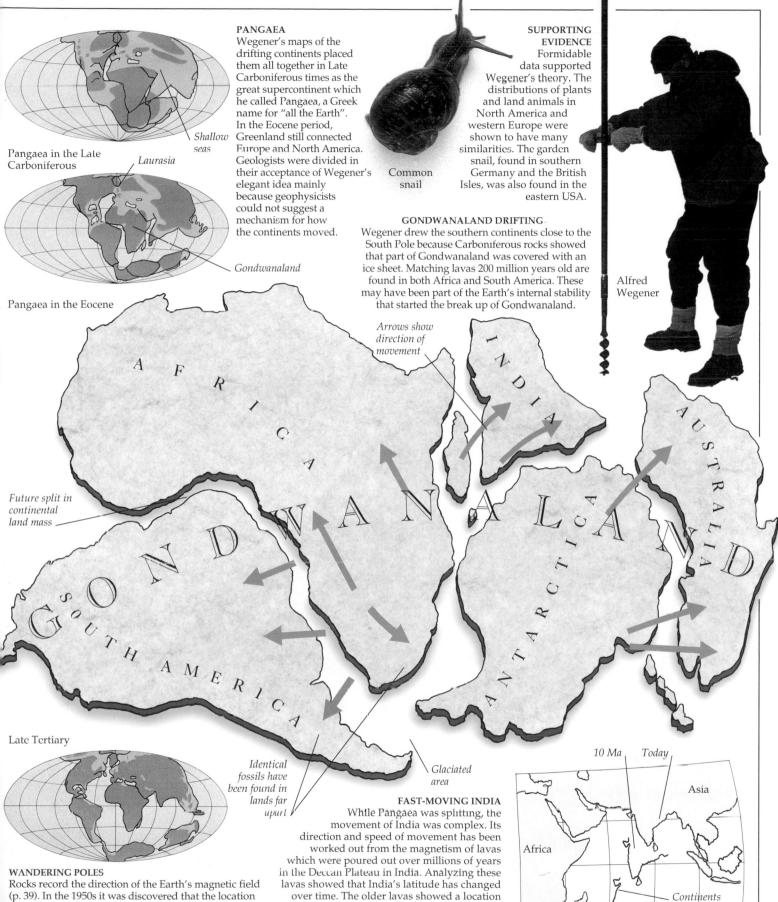

Arrows show direction of movement

Future split in continental land mass

Identical fossils have been found in lands far apart

Glaciated area

Late Tertiary

WANDERING POLES

Rocks record the direction of the Earth's magnetic field (p. 39). In the 1950s it was discovered that the location of the magnetic poles had changed over geological time, and that the pathway along which the pole appeared to wander was not the same in individual continents. This proved that the continents were moving relative to each other at the same time as the poles were moving – thus supporting Wegener's continental drift hypothesis.

FAST-MOVING INDIA

While Pangaea was splitting, the movement of India was complex. Its direction and speed of movement has been worked out from the magnetism of lavas which were poured out over millions of years in the Deccan Plateau in India. Analyzing these lavas showed that India's latitude has changed over time. The older lavas showed a location around 60°S. India then moved rapidly north travelling at 25 mm (1 in) per year, until it began to collide with Asia 55 million years ago, at which time Asia extended further south than today (p. 49). This lost land is now crushed up into the Tibetan Plateau.

10 Ma   Today

Asia

Africa

Continents begin to collide

India moving north

60°S

Plate tectonics

Global relief image of the topography of the South Pole and the Pacific, Indian and Antarctic Oceans

FORTY YEARS AFTER ALFRED WEGENER put forward his controversial continental drift theory (pp. 34-35), technological advances revealed a great deal of information about the ocean floor (pp. 38-39). The discovery of magnetic stripes by two British research scientists F. Vine and D. Matthews in 1963 suggested that the ocean floor was made of younger rock than the continents. This led to the all-embracing theory of plate tectonics which divides the world into plates, made up partly of continent and partly of ocean. For example, the South American plate includes half the south Atlantic Ocean, as well as the continental mass of South America. New plate is being made all the time at spreading ridges (the submarine mountains found by *Challenger*, p. 30) in the oceans, and old oceanic plate material is being recycled in subduction zones. In the process of subduction (p. 43), some oceanic sediments and even whole islands are added on to the continents. Plate tectonics also helps to explain the coincidence between lines of volcanoes, deep ocean trenches, and the location of earthquakes.

AN ALTERNATIVE THEORY
In 1931 British geologist Arthur Holmes (1890-1965) came up with the idea for a mechanism which might allow land masses to move. He suggested that hot currents rising under the oceanic ridges and descending at the edges of the continents were responsible for the continents' movements. He had no observations at this time to support his theory. Holmes was also a pioneer of radiometric dating (pp. 60-61).

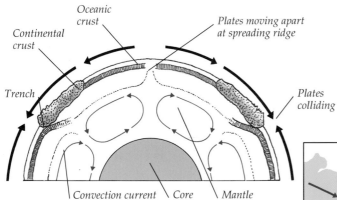

THE MOVING PLATES
There is still controversy about what moves the plates over the surface of the Earth. Possibly, convection currents in the mantle help to push them. Heat rises and convection occurs as heat is lost from the core to the mantle. The currents move very slowly, and carry the plates along. As cooled mantle descends, it is replaced by new hot mantle. Scientists believe that the mantle is unresponsive to short-term events, like the sudden shock of earthquake waves passing through, but in response to long-term stress, applied over tens of millions of years, it can move by slow flow. The mantle slowly evolves as it convects, giving up some of its substance to magmas which make up new edges of plate.

PLATE TECTONIC MAP OF THE WORLD
Plate boundaries, or margins, divide up the surface of the Earth. Some pass very close to the junctions between continents and oceans, but the great majority bear no relationship to the edges of the continents. The Australian plate contains Australia and a large part of the Indian Ocean, as well as other surrounding oceans. Today, all oceanic crust is less than 200 million years old. It has solidified from magma over this time at the spreading ridges (pp. 38-39). Any older oceanic crust has been consumed in subduction zones (p. 43). By contrast, the continents are very old (pp. 40-41).

KEY TO MAP

Destructive plate boundary

Constructive plate boundary

---- Uncertain plate boundary

→ Direction of plate movement

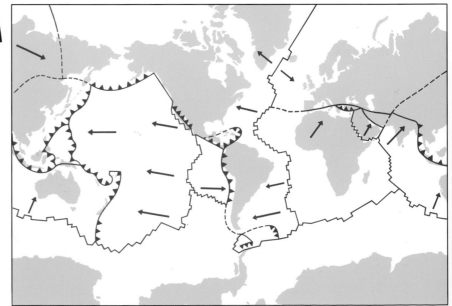

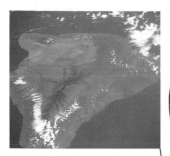

HOT SPOT VOLCANO
Hawaii, with some of the most active volcanoes in the world, is not at a plate boundary. There are isolated places within oceanic or continental plates where magma erupts through the thickness of the plate (pp. 44-45). This is called a hot-spot.

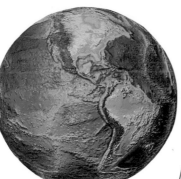

Global relief map of North and South America

SAN ANDREAS REGION
At some plate boundaries, the plates slide past one another, in opposing directions or in the same direction at different speeds. There is no mechanism to produce magma, so there are no volcanoes. This is a boundary where plate is neither made nor destroyed (pp. 42-43).

ICELAND
At constructive plate boundaries, new oceanic plate is being made as magma emerges from the mantle. It fills a widening rift left as the plates move apart. Iceland is made of oceanic crust material even though it is above sea level (pp. 38-39).

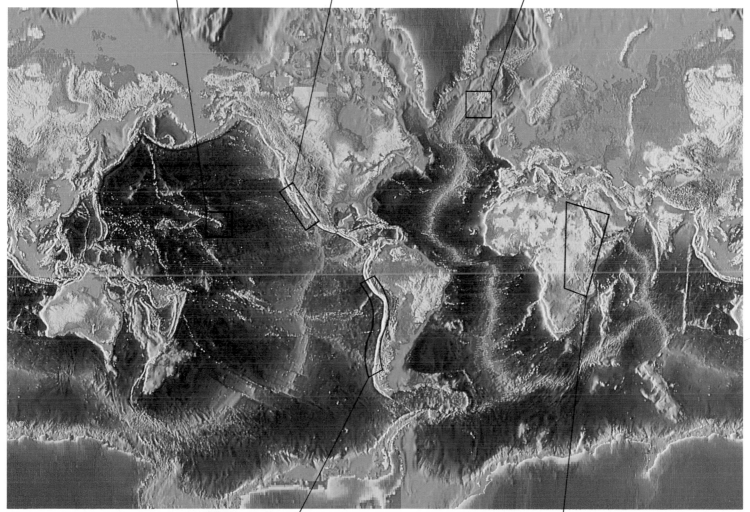

ANDES IN CHILE
Volcanoes, deep ocean trenches, and earthquakes occur at the destructive plate margins called subduction zones. Here, oceanic plate is consumed or destroyed as it goes down into the mantle and is over-ridden by the neighbouring plate (pp. 42-45).

AFRICAN RIFT VALLEY
Continents begin to split apart along rift valleys. In Africa, a branching rift extends southwards from the Red Sea. This area was uplifted some 20 million years ago, and lava erupted. There are still many active volcanoes in this rift valley (pp. 48-49).

Map of mid-Atlantic Ridge

The formation of the ocean floor

HARRY HESS (1906-1969)
An American geologist, Hess worked in submarines during the Second World War where he was mapping the topography of the ocean floor. He found that the heat flowing from the ocean floor was much greater than expected. In 1960 he suggested that the ocean floor was young, because of the hot mantle rock continually rising and crystallizing at the ridges. He argued that the ocean floor was moving away from the ridges and was being consumed back into the mantle at the ocean trenches which surround the Pacific Ocean.

THE SURVEY SHIP *Challenger* (pp. 30-31) discovered that most of the ocean floor lies around 5 km (3 miles) below the level of the sea. This deep ocean floor is all made of relatively young rocks, none older than 200 million years. There was ocean floor in earlier times, but all of that old rock has disappeared, subducted into the Earth's interior at destructive plate boundaries (pp. 36-37). New ocean floor is being made all the time by sea-floor spreading, which takes place at mountainous volcanic ridges. Here, magma rises from the mantle and fills the crack left as the ocean floor pulls apart. The uppermost layer of the volcanic ocean floor is basalt lava. Beneath this is a layer with vertical structures, and below this a third layer made of coarse-textured gabbro. The Earth's magnetic field reverses its direction from time to time, and these reversals are recorded in the new ocean floor rocks as they crystallize.

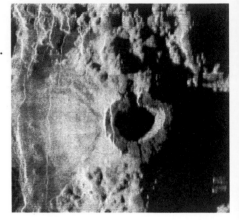

OCEAN-FLOOR VOLCANO
This sonar image shows a volcano on the Mid-Atlantic Ridge. Some ocean-floor volcanoes are active and produce enough lava to make islands. Others, like this one, are well below sea level. A third extinct type have flat tops, and are called guyots. Their tops were once at sea level, where the waves planed them flat. The ocean floor moved away from its spreading ridge, cooling and contracting as it moved, carrying the guyot into deeper water.

BLACK SMOKERS
Hot springs at the spreading ridges emit water heated by the underlying magma. This water is sea water that has seeped into the new hot ocean floor as it cracks during cooling. The water gets hotter as it circulates through the hot rock, enabling it to dissolve more and more minerals from the rock it travels through. When the water is boiled out at the rift in the spreading ridge, it is full of metal sulphides in solution. As these come into contact with cold sea water, they come out of solution as black particles that build up into a smoker, a chimney-like structure that supports specially adapted animals (p. 10).

Kayangel Atoll in the Pacific Ocean

Manganese nodule

CORAL ATOLLS
Coral atolls are ring-shaped islands constructed by reef-building corals. Charles Darwin (1809-1882) showed them to be reefs around the fringes of extinct volcanic islands that had sunk below wave level. Many of these sunken islands turned out to be guyots – flat-topped mountains in the deep ocean. Harry Hess investigated why some guyots had no coral fringe. He realized that they sank beneath the depth of wave erosion (p. 54) as they were transported away from the hot, high ridges and some had sunk too fast for coral building to keep pace.

MINING THE OCEAN FLOOR
The deep ocean floor is littered with rounded nodules which contain the metal manganese. They are especially common where sediment collects only slowly. They grow gradually by adding another skin of metal around the outside and may join together as here. Measurements of the ages of the rings from radiometric dating (p. 61) show that nodules grow extremely slowly. Their origin is in debate, but the metal content suggests maybe there is a connection with the metal sulphides of black smokers (above).

Mapping the ocean

Following the invention of echo-sounding techniques a ship can chart the water depth as it travels. More sophisticated depth recording in the 1950s mapped the ocean floor and showed the diversity of the topography for the first time. The soundings revealed volcanoes, rivers, trenches and spreading ridges – the longest continuous mountain chain on the Earth, stretching 65,000 km (40,400 miles).

The Mid-Atlantic Ridge is above sea level in Iceland

THE MID-ATLANTIC RIDGE

This model of a section of the Mid-Atlantic Ridge was made from sonar images that map the ocean floor precisely. A series of parallel ridges develop as the rift valley cracks and widens, each length of rift wall slumping into the rift. In the centre, the rift is shown at its deepest. The red represents hot lava welling up from the underlying mantle. Individual sections of the central rift are offset sideways by transform faults. These transform, or move, the ridge from one place to another.

Central rift

Black smokers occur in cooler areas

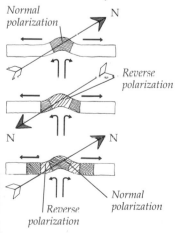

ABOVE SEA LEVEL IN ICELAND

The amount of magma coming from the mantle under Iceland is so great that a huge thickness of lava has built up the Icelandic land mass. Here, the ridge is above sea level. The central feature of the ridge in Iceland is a rift valley where volcanic activity is greatest.

Rift valley

Transform fault

Plate movement

Hot magma

HOW OCEAN FLOOR FORMS

Hot magma wells up under a crack – a rift valley – in the ocean. Some of the magma wells right up to the sea bed and crystallizes as basalt lava. Some solidifies in the rift valley itself, making a vertical wall parallel to the length of the rift valley. Some solidifies more slowly below.

Normal polarization

N

Reverse polarization

N

N

Normal polarization

Reverse polarization

MAGNETIC STRIPES

Basalt lava contains minerals which align themselves in the direction of the Earth's magnetic field as they crystallize. The Earth's field reverses its direction from time to time, and the lavas preserve the direction of the field for the time when they crystallized. Over a long period, a whole series of stripes recording normal and reversed polarity events makes up the ocean floor (p. 61).

Parallel ridge

Deepest part of rift

Parallel ridge

Antarctica

PLOTTING PLATE MOVEMENTS

This satellite image shows the topography, or shapes and structures, over a vast area of the ocean floor between Antarctica and South America. The conspicuous parallel ridges are old parts of the spreading ridge that surrounds the continent of Antarctica. Geologists use these shapes to work out the age and past movements of the plates.

Exploring the interior

Subterranean world as imagined in 1665

THE EARTH'S INTERIOR may forever remain inaccessible (p. 32), but indirect methods have revealed that it has a layered structure with an inner and outer core, surrounded by a mantle, and a crust around the outside. In 1910 a Croatian scientist, Andrija Mohorovicic (1857-1936), concluded after studying transmission of waves from a local earthquake that there was a boundary about 35 km (21 miles) down. This is now called the Mohorovicic Discontinuity after him – shortened to Moho – and it marks the base of the crust. There are clues to the nature of the mantle and outer core. Volcanic eruptions bring some samples of mantle rocks to the surface and the chemistry of the mantle can be guessed at from the chemistry of basalt lavas which originate by partial melting of the mantle. Other indicators include earthquake waves, which travel at variable speeds through the interior of the Earth, depending on the density of the rock they pass through. Some kinds of waves are cut off altogether in the outer core, indicating it is liquid as far as wave transmission is concerned, in spite of huge pressure there. By looking at the changes in the orbits of the planets and their moons as well as those of space satellites, it has been shown that the Earth's greatest mass is concentrated in the core.

HEAT FROM BELOW
Hot springs, which erupt violently as geysers, are visible proof that temperature increases with depth inside the Earth's crust. Miners have known this for many centuries. In the deepest modern gold mines in South Africa, the geothermal heat is so intense that the mines must be cooled in order to permit any human activity at all.

Solid iron inner core
Heavy silicates
Liquid iron outer core

Continental crust
Continental shelf
Ocean crust
Sea level
Lithosphere
Base of lithosphere
Moho
Mantle

LAYERED EARTH
The plates that move around on the Earth's surface are made of more than the thickness of the crust. They include the uppermost part of the mantle. The plate is called lithosphere and is everywhere about 100 km (62 miles) thick. Oceanic lithosphere has oceanic crust at the top, which is only about 5 km (3 miles) thick. Continental lithosphere has continental crust above, which is thicker – 35 km (21 miles).

USING SEISMIC WAVES
Earthquake waves travel through the Earth, and their travel times can give information about the structure of the material they pass through. Vibrations can also be produced artificially to investigate inaccessible rocks at shallow depths. These special trucks give out a restricted range of vibrations. These are picked up by listening devices called geophones situated various distances away.

Trucks send out vibrations

Red garnet

GARNET PERIDOTITE
Garnet peridotite, which has approximately the same density as the mantle, is found at the Earth's surface. Volcanic diamond-bearing rocks called kimberlite contain garnet peridotite. To make diamond, high pressure is needed, equivalent to a depth of around 150 km (93 miles) inside the Earth, so maybe the garnet peridotite fragments in the kimberlite are portions of the mantle from the same great depth.

Eclogite  Granite

Eclogite is found deep in the crust

Eclogite on scales

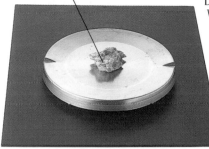

Weight in grams

1 WEIGH THE ROCK
The sample of eclogite is first weighed.

2 MEASURE VOLUME
To determine the volume of a rock for density calculation, a Eureka jar is filled with water up to the point where water flows out of the spout. The rock is then put gently inside. The volume of water displaced through the spout is equivalent to the volume of the rock in cubic centimetres.

DENSE ROCKS
We cannot look at or touch the Earth's mantle directly, but some surface rocks have the same density, so maybe they have come from the mantle. The density of a rock gives a guide to what it might be made of. Crustal rocks from the continents on average have a density like that of granite, around 2.8. Mantle rocks are much denser at 3.3. To find the density of a rock, the mass of the rock is compared to an equal volume of water.

Eclogite inside Eureka jar

Displaced water pours out into beaker

SIR WILLIAM LOGAN (1798-1875)
Travelling through uncharted terrain, the Canadian geologist Logan first mapped the very old rocks of the Canadian Shield (an area that has remained stable). He realized their great antiquity and that they represented rocks from the deepest levels of the Earth's crust. It is believed these rocks, which make up the antique cores of continents, may underlie all the younger continental rocks. Knowledge of deep-level rocks is still sketchy, based on seismic work (p. 42), and on comparisons with the complicated metamorphic rocks (pp. 28-29) of the shield.

Lake Bonneville, Salt Lake City, Utah, USA

BALANCING ACT
The thick, heavy ice sheets of the Pleistocene Ice Age depressed the surface rock layers of the crust beneath, and some of the mantle flowed out of the way. When the ice melted, the crust was unloaded and the mantle slowly flowed back to compensate for the loss of mass. The mantle flowed more slowly than the ice was melting, so Scandinavia is still rising today. This effect of the natural balancing between material of higher and lower density is called isostasy.

FLOATING CITY
Isostasy acts slowly, because the mantle flows slowly. Isostatic readjustment can be seen at the salt flats of Lake Bonneville, where Salt Lake City is built. The salt flats were once occupied by a vast, deep lake, which has been considerably reduced. The area is still rising in isostatic adjustment to the removal of the weight of the water.

The weight causes the wood to float low in the water

The crust is depressed by the ice sheet like the wood with a weight on top

The weight is removed

The wood floats low in the water

The continents float on the mantle like the wood on the water

The wood pops up

Earthquakes and seismology

JAPANESE INSTABILITY
Japan lies over a destructive plate boundary and consequently has many volcanic eruptions and great earthquakes. The land is rapidly being uplifted, making mountains, which themselves are rapidly eroding. Japanese people live with continual upheaval and change of their landscapes.

MOST LARGE EARTHQUAKES HAPPEN at plate boundaries, though a significant number originate in the middle of continental plates (p. 36). The majority of earthquakes go unnoticed by humans. In the build-up to an earthquake, stress accumulates in a volume of rock. The stress comes about because of the movement of the plates, whether slipping past one another or one plate subducting under the continental crust. At the point and time where stress exceeds the strength of the rock, fracture takes place. The fracture travels out through the region of stressed rock, and energy is released in all directions as seismic waves. Seismographs to measure earthquake shaking are highly sensitive devices, capable of recording earthquake waves from the far side of the globe. The traces recorded on seismographs can be read by seismologists to determine the location of a distant earthquake (its epicentre) and how energetic it was (its Richter magnitude). Intensity, based on the Mercalli scale, is compiled from eyewitness reports and from estimates of the response of buildings.

EDUARD SUESS (1831-1914)
An Austrian geologist, Suess theorized about mountain ranges and their relationships to each other. He did not believe that the Earth had evolved through a series of catastrophes. He saw the continents as stable regions, making exception for the seismic zones where earthquakes occur.

Clock mechanism stops when shaking starts

RECORDING EARTHQUAKES
Early seismographs included a device for picking up the shaking. In addition, it was necessary to keep a written record of the shaking as well as to note the moment of arrival of the first tremor and the duration of shaking. The principle of a seismograph is that the recording part moves with the Earth, but a massive part of the apparatus stays stationary. In early equipment, the heavy, huge mass sometimes weighed many tonnes. Modern apparatus is small and inconspicuous and uses electronic circuitry.

Ticker tape shows reading

GROUND CRACKS
Many people imagine that in an earthquake the ground cracks open and people or animals are swallowed up. This is rare but there is sometimes cracked ground, and sometimes ground may liquefy during shaking, especially where the underlying rocks are loosely packed sediments and are saturated with water. During liquefaction, heavy buildings may sink into the ground, or buried objects, such as pipelines and even coffins, may rise to the surface. Landslides and avalanches may occur on steep slopes.

The recording apparatus of a seismograph, developed to record earthquakes near Vesuvius in Italy

PRIMARY AND SHEAR WAVES

Earthquake waves travel outwards in all directions. Some penetrate into the Earth, and their speed increases as they meet ever denser rocks so that they travel in curved pathways, and are refracted back up to the Earth's surface. Those that penetrate to the core are slowed down as they pass into the liquid outer core. Of these, the S waves, which transmit by shearing the rocks they pass through, cannot travel through liquids and are cut off. The primary waves (P waves) have a simpler motion so they travel faster and are the first to be recorded by a seismograph.

S wave   *Epicentre*

Core

Refracted wave   *P wave*

SUBDUCTION ZONES

Earthquakes occur   *Subduction zone*   *Oceanic crust*

Earthquakes are concentrated in sloping zones which underlie mountain ranges and island arcs. Plate tectonics (pp. 36-37) explains that these happen where the oceanic crust is carried down (subducted) into the mantle. The greatest depth at which earthquakes originate is 700 km (435 miles). It is assumed that below this depth, the cold descending lithosphere slab has been heated so much in the mantle that it is no longer brittle enough to fracture.

Direction of convection currents

Mantle

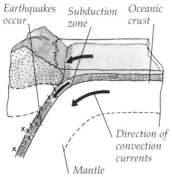

RECORDING EARTHQUAKES

A seismometer records the movement of the ground at strategic points. These readings may be transmitted by radio or telephone line to a recording station. Here a paper record shows one component of the ground motion.

PULLING THE EARTH APART

Some faults occur because rock is under tension. This model (below) shows how faults develop in a series of layered sedimentary rocks. As the layers are stretched, there comes a time when the strength of the rock is no longer able to hold the rock together.

San Andreas fault

The San Andreas plate boundary is a complex of faults about 100 km (62 miles) wide. Here the Pacific plate is moving northwestwards in relation to the land mass of continental North America, so that the relative motion along the boundary is sideways. At these plate boundaries, or margins, plate is neither being made (pp. 38-39), nor consumed.

North America

River has been moved sideways by fault

The San Andreas fault on the west coast of the USA

Fault line   *Highway*

FAMOUS FAULT LINE

Earthquake shaking is less intense the further away it is from the focus, the point where the earthquake originates below the epicentre. Deep earthquakes generally cause less shaking at the Earth's surface above. All the earthquakes on the San Andreas fault are shallow – they originate less than 30 km (19 miles) down.

Transcurrent fault where plates slip past one another

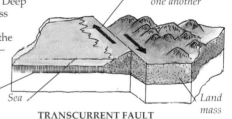

Moving plate   *Sea*   *Land mass*

TRANSCURRENT FAULT

Faults which move predominantly sideways are called transcurrent faults. Along some sections of the fault line, movement is almost continuous. In other places, it appears locked, and stress builds up, leading to a large earthquake.

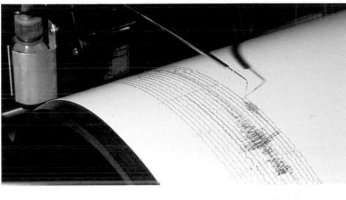

Layers of sand represent sedimentary rock and are coloured so faults can be clearly seen

Fault line

Faulting occurs on either side of rift

Volcanology

THE NAME VOLCANO applies equally to the hole in the ground where lava comes out, as to the mountain built by the eruptions. When lava erupts from a volcano, it is a hot silicate liquid containing gas. Its viscosity varies enormously. Some lava is very fluid and flows freely. Other lavas are so viscous that the lava barely flows at all, and instead heaps up around the hole in the ground and builds a dome. If there is a long time interval between eruptions – say hundreds or even thousands of years – the entire top of the volcano may be blown to dust in a major explosion. Most volcanoes occur in chains that follow the plate boundaries. The formulation of the plate tectonics theory (pp. 36-37) helped to explain the mystery of why volcanoes are not dotted randomly around the globe. Many are to be found around the shores of the Pacific Ocean and in a belt through the Mediterranean to Indonesia. Some volcanoes are at subduction zones (p. 43) where ocean floor moves down into the mantle and is partly melted, making magma (p. 25). Others occur at the spreading ridges where they make new ocean floor (p. 39). Other locations are in rift valleys where continents first began to split apart (p. 49).

Icelandic

Hawaiian

Strombolian

Vulcanian

Pelean

Plinian

THE GRACEFUL MONSTER
Mount Vesuvius in Italy erupted in AD 79. Before the eruption the sides of the volcano were lushly covered in vines. Roman cities on its slopes were engulfed by hot ash. The less-devastating 1872 eruption is shown here.

Long handle allows the volcanologist to stand at a safe distance

The twisted metal hook picks up lava from the flow

COLLECTING LAVA
Many changes take place in lava as it cools and solidifies. Volcanologists (scientists who study volcanoes) watch events during an eruption and collect samples. Sampling helps to understand magma formation and to predict how far flows of lava will travel, and how quickly. This metal rod is used for collecting hot lava.

Twisted shape

CLASSIFYING ERUPTIONS
Eruptions are described according to the explosiveness of their activity. This ranges from the mildest outpourings of syrupy lava, to vigorous eruptions where magma gases escape in intermittent explosions, or in clouds of hot ash.

STUDYING VOLCANOES
Observing at an active volcano can be dangerous. To get close in to the action, special heat-resistant clothing must be worn. While this protects from heat, gas, and falling lava blobs, it also hinders the volcanologist's freedom of movement. To describe an eruption, a volcanologist uses the classifications of eruption type (above right), which are internationally understood. This photograph shows a volcanologist in front of fire fountaining in a Hawaiian-type eruption, taking place in Iceland.

Rough, vesicular surface   Lava bomb

LAVA BOMB
Fragments of lava that are thrown out in fire fountains are still molten as they fly through the air. They cool as they fall, taking on a shape moulded by their flight.

Hawaiian volcanoes

The Hawaiian islands are the tops of a chain of volcanic islands situated over a hot spot in the mantle that has been producing magma for the last 6 million years. The site of volcanic activity at the surface appears to have moved, but actually the hot spot in the mantle stays still; it is the Pacific plate which moves, carrying each volcano northwestwards.

Asia
North America
Pacific Ocean

Hawaiian island chain

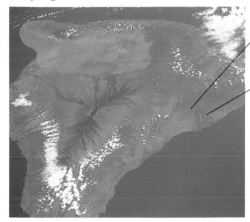

The core of Kilauea

New lava

Ropy lava from a Hawaiian eruption

ROPY LAVA
Highly fluid lava cools with a continuous glassy skin over the surface. The internal flow may push up the cooled skin into wrinkles resembling strands of rope.

Wrinkled surface

EXPLOSIONS
The popular image of volcanoes is a cone-shaped mountain with a crater on top where lava flows out from time to time. In fact, some are mere cracks in the ground, of which many occur in the ocean where lava pours out to cover the seabed. The fast-flowing lava eruptions are less dangerous to humans than those with thick viscous lava which erupt explosively. These can bury towns under thick layers of ash.

THE LARGEST VOLCANO
On the "Big Island" of Hawaii, lava poured from the volcano Kilauea for a decade beginning in the early 1980s. The southern slopes of the island became carpeted with new lava. The island actually grew as lava flowed into the sea, making new land. Above sea level, the whole island makes up only a small fraction of the volcano. The rest is hidden below the sea. The entire volcano is 10,000 m (32,800 ft) high, making it the tallest mountain (from sea floor to summit) on the Earth.

Vesicular lava from a Hawaiian-type eruption

Island arc   *Trench*   *Spreading ridge*   *Volcanic mountain chain*

Hot-spot volcano

Subduction zone

VOLCANOES AND PLATE TECTONICS
Most volcanoes occur at plate boundaries. A few volcanoes, some of them the largest and most active on the Earth, are in mid-plate. These are the hot spot volcanoes. As the plate moves over the hot spot, a chain of volcanic islands forms, getting older the further they are from the hot spot.

Gas bubble (vesicle)

VESICULAR LAVA
When magma erupts, volcanic gas comes bubbling out from the liquid. Bubbles in the middle of the cooling lava cannot escape, so eventually the lava hardens with the gas-filled holes.

Mountain building

GEOLOGISTS ONCE THOUGHT that the folded structures in mountain ranges showed that the Earth was shrinking, and they likened mountain ranges to wrinkles on a shrivelling apple. It is now known that mountain ranges are made up of rocks that have been stacked up and deformed into complicated structures, and that the Earth is not shrinking because new crust is being made in the oceans all the time (pp. 38-39). Usually there is more than one generation of deformation in the making of a mountain range, so that folds become refolded. Broad common features of mountain ranges are that the foothill rocks are recognizably sedimentary (pp. 26-27), while the middle of the ranges have more complicated rocks and structures – these rocks may be intensely deformed and recrystallized (pp. 24-25). Young mountain ranges at active plate boundaries (pp. 36-37) may have volcanoes sitting atop all the deformed structures. There is certainly a great deal of crushing and shortening of the crust in mountain building. However, deformation and uplift in themselves do not create the jagged peaks that are recognizably mountains. Erosion (pp. 54-55) of many kilometres thickness of rock from the top of the rising land mass exposes the deep core of the mountain range. The entire process that makes mountain ranges is called orogenesis.

CROSSING THE ALPS
The Swiss physicist and explorer Horace Benedict de Saussure (1740-1799) crossed the Alps 17 times in different places to try to understand how mountain ranges are created. In the end, he decided that mountains were a hopeless jumble and that to understand their structures was beyond possibility.

Upper parts of fold have been eroded

Sediment layers used to be horizontal

THE ROCKY MOUNTAINS
In the late 19th century it was assumed that some of the crustal shortening of mountain ranges was brought about by one set of rocks being pushed over another set. This is called thrusting, and involves large-scale near-horizontal movements of the upper crustal layers. This seemed a far-fetched idea, but it turned out to be right. The structures in the Rocky Mountains involve multiple thrusting, one mass on another. It is hard to imagine how these great movements could be accomplished in material as hard and brittle as rock. The upper section of rocks that is pushed in thrusting is called a nappe.

The Rocky Mountains on the west coast of North America

FOLD MOUNTAINS
Mountains show layers of sediments that have been folded into complex shapes. These vertical strata in southern England were folded at the same time as the Alps were formed a long way to the south.

Simple deformation of sedimentary rock

Foothills

MODELLING MOUNTAINS

It is hard to understand how the complicated structures which geologists map in the field have come into being. Simplified models of mountain ranges forming from continental collisions can be made in a laboratory. A machine spreads coloured sand in a tank. A paper sheet is rolled slowly underneath the sand, reducing the length of the layers to imitate subduction (p. 43).

Hopper disperses sand

Paper rolled up at measured pace

Paper creates friction under sand

Paper moves 1 cm (½ in) per 100 seconds

Sediments are laid down

First folds

Z-shaped folds develop as the paper is moved at a steady rate

Second Z folds

New folds begin to form; the first set are more intensely deformed

Three nappes created, each underlain by a thrust plane

Nappe

FINAL STAGE

A series of thrusts has placed one nappe on top of another. This model only represents part of what happens in nature. In reality, uplifting, folding, and thrusting are accompanied by erosion, intrusions, and volcanoes.

Nappe

Thrust plane

The Andes

There are many signs of continuing uplift and other tectonic activity in the Andes. Many of the world's largest earthquakes originate here. Young marine sediments are found high above sea level, showing that uplift has been rapid. The Andes are distinctive for the large number of active volcanoes which make up many of the highest peaks. These are built above the mountain range itself. The volcanoes have produced great level spreads of ash making up the elevated plateau of the altiplano.

South America

The Andes mountains

MOUNTAINS IN CHILE

The jagged nature of mountains comes about from erosion of land that has been raised by thrusting and deformation in orogenesis.

Mountain range

Continental crust

Sea

Sediments scraped from ocean floor

DESTRUCTIVE PLATE BOUNDARIES

The destructive plate movement in the Andes occurs when oceanic crust subducts beneath the continental crust. Sediments from the ocean floor are scraped off and added to the continent.

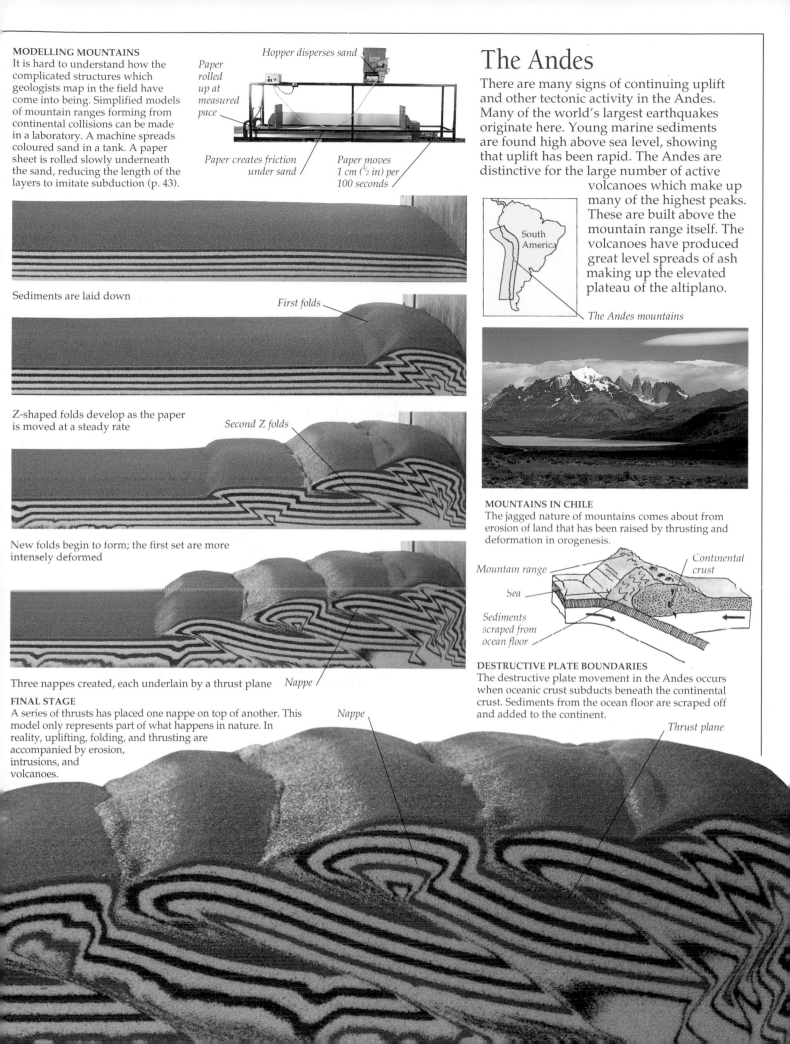

Plateaux and rifts

A TOTALLY NEW PLATE BOUNDARY appears when a continent starts to rift apart. This happened 200 million years ago when the Atlantic Ocean first began to grow (pp. 38-39). Today, the continent of Africa is splitting apart along the African Rift Valley to make a new plate boundary. Not all rift valleys become oceans. Some remain as rifts to fill up with thick layers of igneous rocks and sediments. Some plateaux form when continents collide with each other. This happens when there is no more oceanic crust between them to be subducted. Unlike oceanic crust, continental crust does not subduct because it is too light in weight. So if the edges of continents collide, there is major crushing instead of one plate slipping under the other, and this forms a high plateau like the Tibetan Plateau. Other plateaux come about by gentle raising of a whole region.

AUSTRIAN CANYON
A canyon is a deep valley with vertical sides that has been worn away and eroded by river water. The Austrian Alps show many such slot-like canyons in limestone.

JOHN WESLEY POWELL (1834-1902)
Powell was an American who explored the Grand Canyon in 1869. He had lost his right arm in the Civil War, but managed to climb the canyon walls in places and helped navigate his boats through the fast-flowing waterways.

RIFTING MODEL
The laboratory model below demonstrates the results of rifting. The layers show the fractures which cause rift valleys, sometimes with several more or less parallel faults, each of which allows the rift area to drop further down. The rift section is sometimes known as a graben. In between the dropped blocks are regions which have stayed high. These are called horsts.

THE GRAND CANYON
The great thickness of sediments that make up the Colorado Plateau have been lifted 3,000 m (9,840 ft) over the last 60 million years. Powell's team realized that the Grand Canyon showed no signs of glaciation. The only explanation was that the river had eroded out the huge canyon, cutting first through the softer sediments and – at the bottom of today's canyon – through metamorphic rocks and granites.

Red and white sand shows the sedimentary layers formed at the same time as rifting

Horst

Graben

African Rift Valley

Running through east Africa from Mozambique to the Red Sea is a great rifted valley which branches into two parts. Here Africa is splitting apart along faults where the continental lithosphere (p. 40) has broken right through. Young, active volcanoes and many earthquakes show that the rift is active. At the north, where the Rift Valley joins the Red Sea at the Danakil Depression, the floor of the rift is below sea level and made of oceanic crust, but it is still land. Further south, none of the rock in the African section has oceanic crust. Sometime in the future, a new ocean may separate eastern Africa from the rest of the continent.

Mountains / *Plateau lake* / *Plateau lake*

Satellite antenna

Africa

The African Rift valley

Danakil Depression

THE TIBETAN PLATEAU
The highest, level region on Earth is the Tibetan Plateau at 4,500 m (14,760 ft) above sea level. It is surrounded by young mountains to which its origins are linked. Other plateaux, like some in Africa, are not close to young mountain ranges; they seem to have formed from simple uplift.

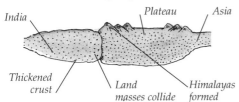

India / *Plateau* / *Asia*

Thickened crust / *Land masses collide* / *Himalayas formed*

CRUNCHING LAND MASSES
During the last 10 million years, India has moved northwards into Asia after the total subduction (p. 43) of the Tethys Ocean that lay between the two land masses. As they collided, Asia became compressed, deformed and fractured, creating the Himalaya mountains. The interior began to compress to make the Tibetan Plateau.

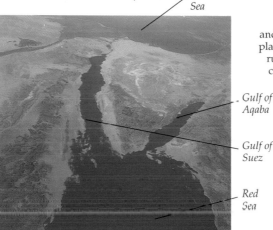

Mediterranean Sea

Satellite view of the Gulfs of Suez and Aqaba and the Red Sea

Gulf of Aqaba

Gulf of Suez

Red Sea

KENYAN RIFT SECTION
Rift valleys have volcanoes within the rift, and usually great spreads of basalt lava on the plateau-like areas on either side. The faultlines running along the Great Rift Valley in Kenya can be clearly seen in this aerial photograph.

A MINIATURE OCEAN
Gravity and magnetic surveys of the Red Sea revealed that the submarine sediments were underlain by oceanic crust. Surveys showed there was a pattern of magnetic stripes (p. 39) parallel to the length of the Red Sea; from these the spreading rate can be calculated as 25 mm (1 in) per year. As the Red Sea spreads, so Arabia is moving northeastwards, away from Africa and closing up the sea of the Persian Gulf.

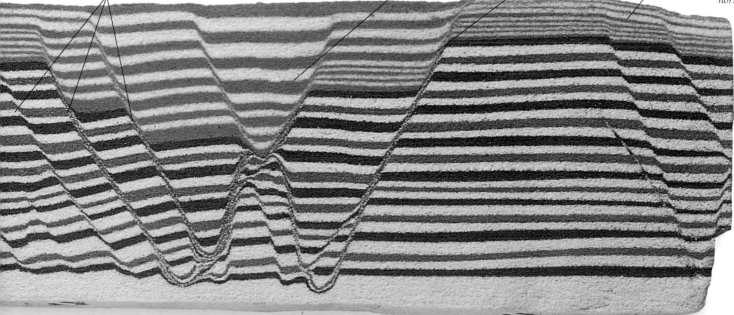

Parallel faults

Thickened red and white layers in the graben

Fracture

Thinner sediment layers on uplifted horst

Weathering processes

Weathering processes leave the landscape with strange shapes

MANY OF THE MINERALS in rocks are stable at the high temperatures and pressures deep in the crust (pp. 40-41) but are chemically unstable in the oxygen-rich atmosphere of the Earth. Rocks react chemically with the Earth's damp atmosphere in a process called weathering, which takes place right at the Earth's surface. This process contributes to the landforms all around. Some weathering is purely chemical – for example, the action of acid rain on limestone (p. 17). Temperature also may play a role in weathering. During the day, rock may be heated by the Sun. When the temperature drops at night, this change leads to stresses and cracking in the rocks. This will be made more extreme if water freezes in the cracks (pp. 58-59). Plants and animals, lichens and fungi also help these processes along. None of these effects, however, happens in isolation. Most landscapes are the result of a combination of many weathering processes. Rock minerals are separated and changed by weathering; this weathered material may be transported and deposited somewhere else (pp. 56-57).

PLANT ACTION
Plant roots penetrate through cracks in rock, and take in rock chemicals to use in their metabolism. As roots grow thicker and the plant bigger, so rock cracks are widened and prised apart. Trees help weathering. So do mosses and lichens, which have fungal roots that can penetrate the hardest rocks.

ANIMAL ACTION
Animals such as rabbits and badgers, as well as smaller creatures like beetles, burrow and make channelways in the weathered rock zone where solid rock comes into contact with moist air. This increases the rate of weathering, because it increases the surface area of the rock. This weathered rock is called saprolite.

RUSTING ROCK
Isolated hills, relics of an older, higher surface, stand above a new younger land surface which is almost a level plain. These isolated mountains are known as inselbergs. The red colour of Uluru (Ayers Rock) in central Australia is due to iron oxides, the insoluble part left behind after silicates are broken down by the Australian climate.

CHANGES IN TEMPERATURE
The rocks in these Utah canyons in the USA are weathered by temperature, wind, and water. Changes in temperature cause cracking as the rocks expand and shrink. If an area gets very cold and freezing follows rain, the rain water which has percolated into cracks and in between rock grains expands as it freezes, breaking the rock apart.

Hay Tor on Dartmoor, southern Britain

LIMESTONE WONDER
Limestone is weathered by carbon dioxide in rain water so that the rock is slowly eaten away. When water carrying the dissolved limestone drips from the roof of a cave, a stalactite forms. If the soil above the cave is an iron-rich clay, the stalactite may be red in colour.

Two stalactites have grown into one

Joint planes develop and weathering takes place

Erosion leaves corestones

Granite tor

GRANITE TOR
Cooled granite eventually comes to the surface when a mountain range is being eroded away; the granite cracks apart as the load of rock over the top gets less and less. In places, the cracks, called joints, are widely spaced apart. In other places, they are close together. Weathering of granite is most intense where the joints are closely spaced. This leaves rounded corestones of unweathered granite, some of which may be several metres or even tens of metres across. The more solid rock stands out as high areas of bare rock known as granite tors.

LIMESTONE LAGOON
The stalactites in this cave on Phra Nang Peninsula, Thailand, were exposed to daylight when the cave collapsed. If the limestone dissolved in water grows up from the floor of the cave, it is known as a stalagmite.

ONION SKINS
Weathering begins on the outside of a rock where it has greatest contact with the atmosphere. Weathering processes penetrate at least 1 cm (½ in) into the rock, even where erosion is rapidly removing the weathered grains. On some rocks, several skins of weathered rock can be seen peeling off from the underlying, more solid rock. This type of weathering is sometimes called onion-skin weathering, or exfoliation.

Peeling layers

Dolerite rock

Cement comes from the weathering of other rocks

Thin section of sandstone

Blue resin shows pore spaces

PORE SPACES
All sedimentary rocks have spaces between the grains of sediment. This may later fill with mineral cement.

Life from rock

ROCKS WEATHER AT THE SURFACE of the Earth where they come into contact with moist air. As soon as plants take root in the weathered saprolite (p. 50), the process of making soil begins. Factors which govern how soil is formed include climate, vegetation, topography, and the nature of the rock from which the soil is made. As well as the mineral material from rock, soil also contains organic material, known as humus. This includes plant roots, decaying plant and animal matter, micro-organisms, and the organic chemicals that are part of the decomposition of plant and animal matter as fungi and microbes break it down. Animals including snails, and worms are part of the organic matter. Water and air between the particles are a vital part of soil; without them, plants would suffocate or dehydrate. The natural processes which make soil are slow and complex, taking tens of thousands of years. By contrast, soil can be used up rapidly, becoming depleted within as little as a decade.

EARTH MOTHER
In early agricultural civilizations, the fertility of women and the fertility of the soil were seen as two parts of the miraculous continuity of life. In ancient Roman mythology, Proserpina, the daughter of Ceres, the Roman goddess of fruitfulness, was abducted into the underworld where she ate some pomegranate seeds. During the months she was imprisoned, the crops would not grow, animals were no longer fertile and death stalked the land – the months of winter.

TERRACING FOR AGRICULTURE
Artificial terraces, where the hillside is cut into steps, make the slopes easier to farm. They provide land which is level and more convenient to irrigate and plough. Terraces have the added advantage of stabilizing slopes by reducing the rate at which soil is lost from the slope to the valley below. Terracing is commonly found with rice cultivation.

Terraced slopes in Yemen

Terraced slope

SOIL PROFILE
A section dug through soil down to the underlying rock reveals the soil profile. It has a number of distinct layers. The top layer is called the A-horizon. Within this layer, the gardener or farmer digs or ploughs through the topsoil. Below lies the B-horizon which may contain accumulations of mineral matter washed in from the upper layers. The B-horizon has more rock fragments from the underlying parent rock. The C-horizon contains a large percentage of broken and weathered rock from which the overlying soil has been derived.

Brown earth (high humus content)

A-horizon contains organic matter

Chalk weathered away, leaving flint behind

B-horizon with little organic matter

Podzolic soil (found in temperate climates)

A-horizon contains organic matter

B-horizon with little organic matter

C-horizon is the rock layer

Chalk

C-horizon is the rock layer

SOIL, AIR, AND WATER

The way soil particles lump together is important to cultivation. So is the size of the mineral grains. Clay soils hold abundant moisture and nutrients, but water passes through slowly. Plants find it difficult to gain root hold and extract nutrients. Sandy soils have large pore spaces and water washes through so they are relatively poor in nutrients. To investigate the nature of the two soils, the same weight of each soil is placed in a test tube and a measured amount of water is added. The difference in water penetration can be clearly seen. The ideal soil lies somewhere between the two.

Water is quickly absorbed in the air spaces

Water is slow to drain

Sandy soil   Clay soil   Sandy soil   Clay soil

A LIVING ORGANISM

Soil is the interface between life and the rocky part of the Earth. Without it, life would be impossible. It is in the soil that chemical exchanges take place which allow plants to grow. When plants die, they give back their chemical content to the soil. Micro-organisms in the soil (fungi and bacteria) convert dead plant and animal matter into simpler chemicals that enrich the soil. By harvesting a crop, some of the fertility of the soil is taken away. If the soil is to continue to produce crops, it must regain nutrients from rock weathering, or from added fertilizers.

SOIL CREEP

Soil is constantly on the move downhill under the influence of gravity. Animals walking across a slope gently nudge the soil as they go. When it rains, soil is wetted and may move as a mud flow. When it freezes, soil particles move out from the slope. After thawing, these particles settle under gravity lower down the slope. Trees on a hillside often show this movement of the soil. As young saplings, they grow vertically. Gradually the soil creep tips them down the slope until they stick out at an angle. The tree sometimes grows in a curve as it tries to maintain its vertical growth upwards into the light.

Wildflowers

Grass

Snail

Decomposing leaf

Dark humus-rich soil

Slug   *Pebbles*   *Roots*

Erosion

Weathering breaks down rocks to form loose material or rock minerals in solution. Erosion is all the ways in which the material in solution and the loose rock fragments are removed from the location of the original rock and transported to another place, usually under the influence of gravity. Rock material may be carried by water, it may be transported by glacier ice (pp. 58-59), or it may be blown by the wind. The amount of rock fragments carried relates to the speed at which water is travelling, so fast-moving rivers in flood can erode huge amounts of landscape. During erosion and transport, the rock fragments are sorted according to their size and nature. The chemical elements that went into solution may travel as far as the sea, where they make the sea more salty. In temperate climates where it rains often, clay and sand grains are carried away by rain water washing over slopes, and then by rivers. The heaviest rock fragments are dropped first wherever the speed of the river slackens. At coastlines where cliffs meet the sea, the land is continually being eroded.

WATER FALLING
As rivers cut their pathway from the mountains down to sea level, irregularities in the rocks or any change in the pathway can make rapids, a waterfall, or a lake. Waterfalls mark a place in the river's pathway where active erosion is taking place. Waterfalls are also common in valleys which have been glaciated (pp. 58-59).

IRREGULAR COASTLINE
Waves beating on a shore hit headlands first. The waves curve around as they meet shallower water and then break against the sides of the headland. If there are joint planes (p. 51) in the rock, or softer rocks, these are eroded away more rapidly than the hard headland rocks. First, an archway forms. Then, if the roof of the arch caves in, an isolated sea stack is left. Waves which hit the coast at an angle move rock fragments along the shore sideways, sometimes for hundreds of kilometres.

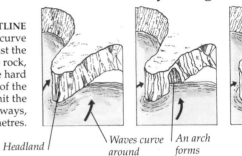

Headland

Waves curve around headland

An arch forms

A sea stack results

CHANGING CLIFF FACE
Waves that meet a steep rocky shore directly break with all their force against the foot of the cliff. Here, solution and weathering happen as salty water continually wets the rock and then dries out at low tide. Salt crystallization occurs and breaks up the grains of the rock. The cliffs are undercut, primarily by wave action, and eventually the upper part falls, breaking along a crack which may be an original joint plane in the rock. The shape of the cliff depends on the resistance of the different rocks to the pounding of the waves.

Man'o War cove, southern Britain

WAVES AS AGENTS OF EROSION
Waves are formed by winds blowing over water. The wave fronts in deep water are parallel to one another. As they meet shallower water, they bend, and hit the shore in a curve. These curved waves affect the shape of the shoreline. The offshore reef on this coastline breaks up the wave energy. The resulting curved wavelets contribute to the characteristic shape of the cove. Each incoming wave moves pebbles and sand along the beach sideways; the backflowing water moves the material back down the beach.

Wave fronts curve

Normandy cliffs, France

Arch

Headland

Sea stack

Massive rock bed has resisted erosion

SALT CRYSTALLIZATION

Pinnacles of rock weathered in a dry climate show hard bands of rock which stand out on the surface. Other layers are more easily weathered and eroded. This uneven sculpting by the weather relates to the changes in grain size and pore size from one rock layer to another. Large pore sizes allow water to penetrate deeply into the rock when it rains. In a dry climate, or where there are high winds, the surface dries before the interior of the rock does. Later, as the soaked-in water dries, salts weathered out from the rock crystallize just under the surface. These push apart the rock grains. The loosened grains are blown away by the wind.

SANDS OF TIME

Weathering in the desert is a result of fracturing brought about by temperature changes and by salt crystallization. Erosion is mostly brought about by the wind which continually blows away the smallest particles and flaky mineral grains, leaving rounded quartz sand. These sand grains are transported a cross the surface of the desert where they form sand dunes. The dunes also move, with sand being blown up the gentle slope and sliding in occasional avalanches down the steep slope.

Sand dune in Morocco

Natural rock arch

Wadi

Slopes are covered with weathering rock fragments

Sand dunes

Rock fragments collect in wadi

MODEL OF A DESERT LANDSCAPE

The notion of deserts as only sandy places is not entirely true. Antarctica (p. 18) is a desert because, like the Sahara, it receives less than 25 cm (10 in) rainfall each year. When torrential rain does come to arid areas, whole mountainsides may be swept clean of boulders, rock fragments, sand, and clay in flash floods which pour down wadis (dry river valleys) to drain into temporary lakes, or playas. The rock fragments which build up in gullies at the foot of steep mountainsides may be weathered to make sand. The sand is washed out, or blown away to make dunes.

Area of rock has eroded more easily

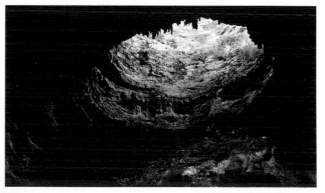

HOLES IN THE RIVER BED

Sometimes rivers disappear underground in caves known as potholes. Some of these are enlarged cracks in limestone, but others are formed by the collapse of the limestone over an underground cave. Limestone weathers and erodes into cave systems if the rock is hard enough to be self-supporting when it is hollowed out. The best limestones for this are fine-grained limy muds (p. 51) which have been cemented together to make a tough rock. More shelly limestones form cave systems less readily.

Deposition

ALL THE ROCK FRAGMENTS broken off from the solid rocky surface of the Earth are deposited somewhere else as sediment. The environment of deposition varies enormously, and this controls the character of the sediment. If the circumstances are just right, the sediments may eventually become new sedimentary rocks. The environments of deposition vary from steep mountain slopes, to flat river valleys, to beaches, to the seabed on the continental shelf, and to the deep ocean floor. Many sediments that are laid down are eroded again fairly soon afterwards. This might happen as pebbles are dropped after a river flood and then picked up and transported further downstream in the next flood. During this time, the pebbles and other grains undergo weathering as well as further transport. The best place for sediments to be made into rock is a location where the land surface is sinking, or where the sea level is rising. Under these circumstances, one sediment layer is rapidly buried by another and is preserved. Once buried, it becomes compressed and hardened to make rock.

Vale of Glamorgan coast, Wales

SHAPING THE BEACH
Coastal beaches are places of continual change (p. 54). The nature of the waves breaking on this beach causes the banks of pebbles to be scoured and sorted. However, even beaches have definite seasonal cycles. Sand moves on to the beach in summer, while in winter the high waves usually pick the sand up and deposit it offshore.

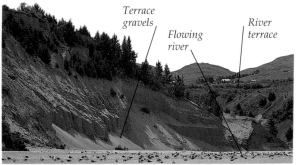

Terrace gravels

Flowing river

River terrace

Shotover River, New Zealand

RIVER TERRACES
When a river falls in response to a drop in sea level, the level of the old flood-plain is abandoned above the flowing river. These new incised banks are known as terraces. The terraces are made of older sands and gravel that were previously part of the river bed.

MEANDERING RIVER
The flatter parts of river valleys are where the river drops the load of sediment it has collected from the fast-flowing hilly portion of its pathway. Meandering river valleys are sometimes flat and wide. The river moves in snakelike fashion, the course changing with every flood to make great loops. If the river cuts through the neck of the loop the abandoned loop is known as an ox-bow lake.

Mara River, Tanzania

Deposition of sediment on the inside of the curve

Neck of loop

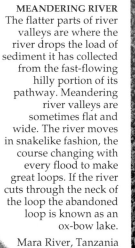

Erosion on the outside of the curve

RIVERS OF SAND
Erosion dominates in the steep parts of the river and deposition dominates in the flood plain area. The river erodes its banks on the outside of a bend where the flow is fastest, and the sediment is redeposited on the insides of bends where the flow is slow. In this way, meandering rivers build wide flat valleys, called flood plains, made from their deposited material.

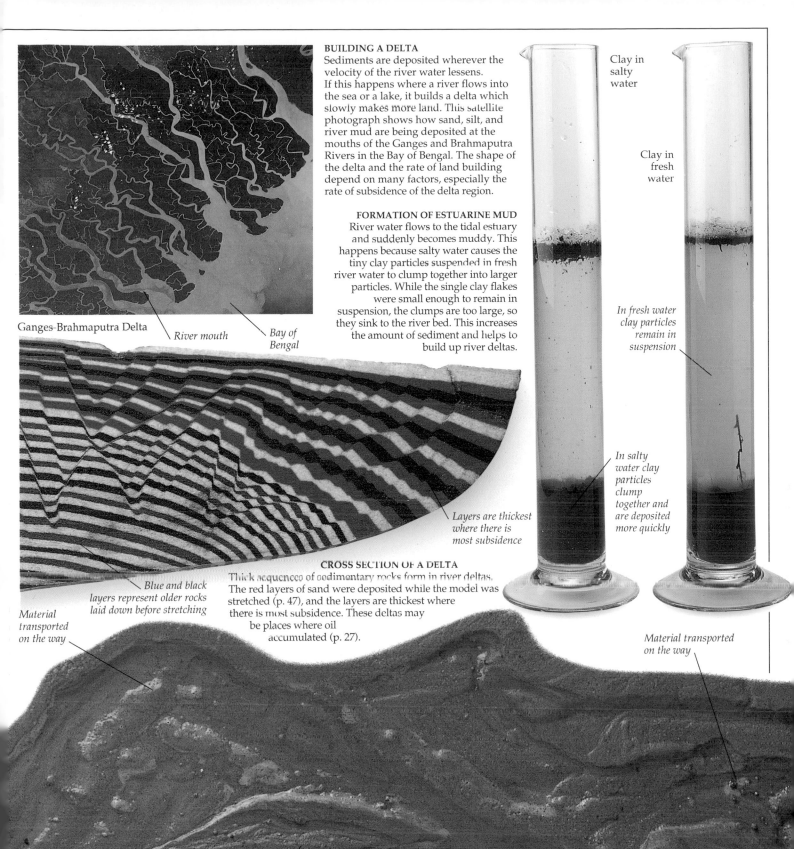

BUILDING A DELTA

Sediments are deposited wherever the velocity of the river water lessens. If this happens where a river flows into the sea or a lake, it builds a delta which slowly makes more land. This satellite photograph shows how sand, silt, and river mud are being deposited at the mouths of the Ganges and Brahmaputra Rivers in the Bay of Bengal. The shape of the delta and the rate of land building depend on many factors, especially the rate of subsidence of the delta region.

FORMATION OF ESTUARINE MUD

River water flows to the tidal estuary and suddenly becomes muddy. This happens because salty water causes the tiny clay particles suspended in fresh river water to clump together into larger particles. While the single clay flakes were small enough to remain in suspension, the clumps are too large, so they sink to the river bed. This increases the amount of sediment and helps to build up river deltas.

Clay in salty water

Clay in fresh water

In fresh water clay particles remain in suspension

In salty water clay particles clump together and are deposited more quickly

Ganges-Brahmaputra Delta

River mouth

Bay of Bengal

Layers are thickest where there is most subsidence

CROSS SECTION OF A DELTA

Thick sequences of sedimentary rocks form in river deltas. The red layers of sand were deposited while the model was stretched (p. 47), and the layers are thickest where there is most subsidence. These deltas may be places where oil accumulated (p. 27).

Blue and black layers represent older rocks laid down before stretching

Material transported on the way

Material transported on the way

A bar is left where the river takes a short cut

River flows faster through short cut

Glaciation

GLACIERS ARE FOUND IN THE HIGH VALLEYS of many mountain ranges today, although most are melting faster than they are replenished by snowfall. This means the valley end of the glacier is continually retreating higher up the mountain. Today's mountain glaciers are but a small leftover from the great glaciers that filled the valleys in the cold stages of the Pleistocene Ice Age. Ten thousand years ago glaciers started to melt faster than they were supplied with snow. It must have taken the same sort of time for the glaciers to build up. Over the last 2 million years, glacier build-up has happened each time a cold, wet, glacial period followed a warmer, interglacial period. The Earth today is thought to be in an interglacial period of glacier melting. As valley glaciers flow, they carve their valleys wider and deeper, eventually making a U-shaped trough. Melting glaciers are hemmed in by great mounds of sediments which were washed out of the ice. These fragments have been scoured or plucked from the surrounding rocks and transported downhill by the glaciers as they move slowly down the valleys. In this way glaciers can transport huge amounts of rock fragments from mountain summits to valley floors.

GLACIER GIANTS
Where a glacier melts at its snout, a tiny water torrent may flow from the bouldery gravel mounds left by the melting ice. The gravel heaps are known as the terminal moraine of the glacier. The great rivers of Europe, such as the Rhine, all have their source in the melting glaciers of the Alps.

CONTINENTAL ICE SHEET
The interiors of Greenland and Antarctica are covered with ice sheets thousands of metres thick. The thickness reduces towards the edge of the land mass. Near the coast of northwest Greenland, valley glaciers are threading their way through mountains which ring the island. Rock fragments are carried along the edges of the glacier (lateral moraines), and also within the ice itself.

Pacific Ocean | *Pack-ice*

SATELLITE SNOWSCAPE
Alaska, Canada, much of the northern USA, and Scandinavia, as well as Antarctica and Greenland, were ice-covered at the coldest stages of the Pleistocene Ice Age. Today, some of these regions are still snow-covered in winter, while only their mountainous regions have permanent glacier ice. In winter, as seen in Alaska from satellite, pack-ice builds up around the coast as the sea freezes and the first winter snow falls. In Siberia, Alaska, and northern Canada, great regions still have permanently frozen ground known as permafrost, though this is reducing in area.

Ice sheet

Terminal moraine

Valley glacier

Crevasse

GREY ICE

During the summer the mature snow on top of glacier ice melts. Dust, either volcanic or blown rock dust, becomes concentrated on the melted surface as a dark veneer (right). The grey snow surface absorbs the Sun's radiation and speeds up summer melting. The winter snowfalls make a new white layer, and in this way dark dust layers mark each summer melt in glacier ice.

Freshly fallen snow

New snow

Névé

Glacier ice

Air squeezed out

Impermeable ice

FROM SNOW TO ICE

Falling snow is made of fluffy flakes which trap air in the new snowfall layer. As the fluffy snow warms and partly melts in daytime and refreezes at night, the crystals grow more compact, with less air between. This more mature snow is called névé. Eventually, what used to be light airy snow is compacted into solid hard ice.

French Alps, near Chamonix

CREATING FIORDS

Glaciers flow slowly and do not easily go round corners, as rivers do. Most grow in existing river valleys, and their flow erodes the sides and floor of the valley. After the glacier melts, what was once a V-shaped meandering river valley has become a straight, U-shaped trough. In mountainous areas near a coastline, the sea flooded into the valleys, many of which are below the new global sea level which rose as the glaciers melted. There are many coastal inlets formed in this way off the west coast of Norway, and so they are known by the Norwegian name, *fjord*. Fiords are also found around the northern continents and in Antarctica and New Zealand .

PLUCKED ROCK

As the glacier passes over a block of rock, some ice melts and trickles into cracks in the rock, where it freezes again. This causes the rock to be plucked off the solid valley floor and carried along by the glacier.

Bedrock

Glacier ice

Plucked boulder

Meltwater seeps into cracks

Scratch marks made by rock fragments trapped in glacier

Boulder clay cemented with lime

Glacial fragments in rock

GLACIER GRATER

The rocky floor over which glacier ice and boulders travel becomes polished by the rock fragments trapped in the flowing glacier. The smoothed surface shows scratches (striae) on pthe surface (left). The glacier transports the fine rock powder that each scratch makes. This powder, along with all the rock fragments, contributes to the glacier's total rock load. The unsorted mass of fine rock powder and small and large rock fragments is left in heaps wherever the glacier melts.This rock is called boulder clay (right), which makes a hummocky landscape.

Limestone rock from Switzerland

Chalky boulder clay

Dating the Earth

JAMES USSHER (1581-1656)
This 17th-century clergyman used biblical evidence to show that the Earth was created in 4004 BC. He based his calculation on the genealogies in the Bible. Ussher's date was believed by many scientists and the general public for a time. Other religions came up with a date for the beginning of the Earth based on their beliefs.

WHEN THINKING ABOUT HOW OLD the Earth might be, James Hutton (p. 8) wrote in 1788 that he could see "no vestige of a beginning, no prospect of an end". Hutton saw geological time as being unimaginably long. It was not until the 20th century, with the understanding of radioactivity, that an accurate method of dating such old materials as Earth rocks was developed. This was radiometric dating which used a measurable Earth process that happened on a time scale of the right order of magnitude. Another method of dating rocks and therefore the age of the Earth is to study layers in sedimentary rocks, and fossils – dead plants and animals that have become preserved in rocks of the Earth's crust. This record in the rocks also helps to reveal past climates, giving information about how the atmosphere used to be on the Earth. The ocean floor preserves the Earth's magnetic field, making a record that goes back 200 million years.

WILLIAM THOMSON (1824-1907)
This British scientist (later Lord Kelvin) calculated the age of the Earth based on the length of time it had taken to cool to its present temperature. He assumed that the Earth originally had a molten surface. The time he came up with was 40 million years. This was far too short to account for the evolution of life or for the accumulation of sedimentary rock strata (p. 62).

USING FOSSILS
The British geologist Charles Lyell (p. 62) realized that young rocks contain many fossils which are similar to living life forms, and that progressively older rocks have fewer and fewer species which resemble modern forms. Palaeontologists who study fossils and stratigraphers who study rock sequences, have compiled an Earth history that allows rocks to be dated from their fossils. For example, *Acadagnostus* is found in Middle Cambrian rocks, while *Eocyphinium* is found in rocks of Carboniferous age.

TIME GAPS
The thickness of rock layers might look like a good way of dating Earth processes, but the rates of sedimentation are difficult to measure. One problem is that the layers contain many time gaps when no strata were laid down or they were eroded. Some gaps represent a very long time interval. From fossils and radiometric dating, the time interval represented at this rock outcrop in southern Britain is 160 million years: the time between when the lower set of rocks was being laid down as sediments, to when it was submerged and buried by new layers of rocks. Such a time gap between deposition of rock layers is called an unconformity.

Acadagnostus

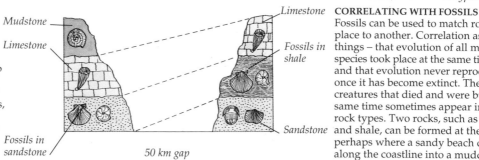

Eocyphinium

Mudstone
Limestone
Fossils in sandstone

Limestone
Fossils in shale
Sandstone

50 km gap

CORRELATING WITH FOSSILS
Fossils can be used to match rocks from one place to another. Correlation assumes two things – that evolution of all members of a species took place at the same time worldwide, and that evolution never reproduces a species once it has become extinct. The fossils of creatures that died and were buried at the same time sometimes appear in different rock types. Two rocks, such as sandstone and shale, can be formed at the same time, perhaps where a sandy beach changed along the coastline into a muddy estuary.

Housing
holding
magnetic
needle

Mirror
to show
movements
of needle

Marble cylinder holds
a pair of coils to produce
a magnetic field

Mineral
sample
placed here

Marble plinth to
isolate the magnet

MAGNETOMETER
Carefully orientated specimens of lava can be collected and taken back to the laboratory. When placed within the magnetic field of a magnetometer, the direction of their magnetic alignment can be determined. This gives a clue to the age of the lava.

Laboratory model of a sedimentary basin

Red and black
layers are
sediments

STRATIGRAPHY – HISTORY THROUGH MAGNETISM
Sedimentary rocks contain grains of magnetic minerals that are weathered from pre-existing igneous rocks. As these grains come to rest in a heap of sediments, each grain orientates itself, like a compass needle, with the Earth's magnetic field (p. 6). So a sequence of sedimentary rocks can be correlated with normal and reversed polarity (p. 39) and compared with their radiometric dates. Some rock types are more suitable than others; red sandstones and shales are particularly useful because they are rich in iron.

TREE RINGS
The age of a felled tree can be calculated by the growth rings in the trunk. Each year is characterized by its own particular growth ring. The oldest trees on the Earth, such as the North American bristle-cone pines, allow these records to be taken back thousands of years. With this information, isolated wood, such as that fossilized within recent lava flows, can be accurately dated.

Amino acids are
extracted from bone
for radiocarbon
dating

RADIOMETRIC DATING
This dating method works from measuring the rate of transformation of one radioactive isotope (parent) to its daughter element. Some radioactive parent/daughter transformations take longer than the age of the Earth. These long-life radioactive elements, such as uranium, are used to date the oldest rocks.

Growth
rings

IN THE LABORATORY
Once an organism dies, its carbon content is no longer being renewed. Radiocarbon dating measures how much carbon 14 is left in a dead organism in relation to carbon 12. In 5,570 years, half of all the carbon 14 in a sample will have changed to carbon 12. This short half-life means that carbon 14 is only suitable for dating wood, bone, and young rocks – those from the last 70,000 years. In this laboratory, a mass spectrometer is being used to sort and count the amounts of each isotope.

Young layers
of wood on
the outside of
the trunk

Fossilized tree trunk

Naming the Earth

T HE MOST RECENT HISTORY of the Earth is the best known, because the younger rocks contain abundant fossils and there is a fairly complete rock record. We know much less about the first 3,000 million years because the rocks contain few and only primitive fossils, and many of the rocks have been metamorphosed several times. Also much of the rock record is either buried by younger rocks or has been eroded to make sedimentary rocks.

CHARLES LYELL (1797-1875)
Lyell's most fundamental contribution to geology was his belief in Uniformitarianism, that "the present is the key to the past". It is now known that this is a decidedly limited truth, as Precambrian history shows. All Earth processes – plate tectonics, mountain building, weathering, sedimentation – had a beginning, probably early in the Precambrian.

THE AGE OF THE EARTH
The Earth is believed to be about 4,550 million years old. This is supported by the age of the oldest rocks on the Moon, and by dating meteorites, which suggests that our Solar System itself may be about this old. Precambrian time includes major events like the origin of the first life forms, the growth of the continents, the beginnings of plate tectonics, and the build-up of atmospheric oxygen.

Stony meteorite

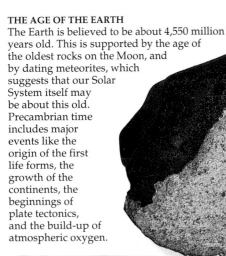

THE PRECAMBRIAN SHIELD
Sir William Logan (p. 40) realized the Precambrian rocks he mapped in the Canadian Shield were enormously old. He called the peculiar structures in these rocks cryptozooans, meaning hidden animal, because these rocks were thought to predate the existence of life.

Paradoxides

SEA SCAVENGERS
The Cambrian marks the time when life became abundant in the oceans and left a clear fossil record of its presence. Trilobites, such as this *Paradoxides,* were bottom dwellers in shallow seas where they scavenged for food.

Mastopora

OXYGEN-GIVERS
Green algae like *Mastopora* produce oxygen in their metabolism and were responsible for releasing oxygen into the atmosphere (p. 10).

Goniophyllum

OLD-LIFE CORALS
Corals like *Goniophyllum* are life-forms that are still familiar.

Pteraspis

OLD ROCK
Much of the first solid crust on Earth was probably like basalt in composition and similar to today's ocean floor. The first granites that make the continents must have come later. Today, Precambrian granites have been metamorphosed, perhaps many times over.

Granite gneiss

Collenia

EARLY LIFE
Collenia are stromatolites – blue-green algae that are one of the earliest forms of life. They usually occur in lumpy pillars between high and low tidal water levels.

BONY FISH
Some life forms have an external skeleton, such as a shell, while others have an internal skeleton. The earliest fish lived in the sea, had an external skeleton of bony plates, and were jawless like this *Pteraspis*.

ARCHAEAN	PROTEROZOIC		CAMBRIAN	ORDOVICIAN	SILURIAN	DEVONIAN
PRECAMBRIAN			PALAEOZOIC			
4,500 Ma	2,500 Ma		590 Ma	500 Ma		400 Ma

EARLY PLANT LIFE

The earliest plant forms are found in Silurian and Devonian rocks. Plants colonized the land in great numbers in the Carboniferous (meaning rich in coal), making up the swamps which later were buried, compressed and heated, and transformed into coal. Club mosses, like this modern *Lycopodium*, first evolved in the Palaeozoic.

Lycopodium

Carboniferous rock

Limy sediment formed in the Jurassic sea

Boreholes made by boring mollusc

BURROWS THROUGH TIME

The grey Carboniferous rock was hardened and eroded. It made a hard rocky seabed in Jurassic times. Shelly molluscs in the Jurassic burrowed into the Carboniferous rock.

ARCHAEOPTERYX

There are so few fossil birds that we know little about their evolution. *Archaeopteryx* is Jurassic in age, and is clearly a feathered bird capable of flying, though still possessing teeth.

Finger

Reptilian tail

Archaeopteryx

Alpine glacier

THE GREAT ICE AGE

One cause of the Ice Age in the Pleistocene epoch (a sub-division of the Quaternary) may be the high mountains, and their locations, which affected global weather systems by diverting surface winds.

DESERT SANDSTONE

Sandstones of Permian age in Europe show they were formed in a desert climate. The sand grains are well-rounded, having been blown around by the wind, and are sometimes in sloping layers (pp. 26-27).

SANDY DESERT

The deserts of Europe must have been as large as the Gobi desert of today. Thick deposits of salt indicate temporary lakes which evaporated in the hot climate. The rocks that formed on the shorelines of these lakes sometimes contain footprints or fossilized skeletons of dinosaurs.

EUROPEAN CHALK

The end of the Mesozoic saw extensive seas in which pure limestone was laid down. The Chalk is made of the shells of tiny algae.

Serrated teeth

Eye socket

Land-dwelling Allosaurus

Cavity for jaw muscles

DINOSAUR FOSSILS

Creatures that lived in the water and dropped to the bottom when they died had a better chance of becoming preserved as fossils. The fossil record is dominated by water-dwelling creatures. Land animals like the meat-eating *Allosaurus* were rarely preserved.

THE ROCKY MOUNTAINS

A high mountain chain was built along the subduction zones on the west of the Americas. Today, global topography is much more varied than is usual in the Earth's history, with many high mountain ranges which are actively being lifted up and eroded (pp. 54-55).

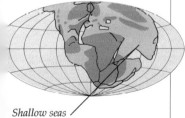

Shallow seas

CARBONIFEROUS MAP

In his map of Pangaea, Alfred Wegener (p. 35) showed all the continents grouped together at the end of Carboniferous times.

RECENT LANDSCAPE

Alfred Wegener's map for late Tertiary times showed the world much as it is today, though with a narrower North Atlantic Ocean. During Tertiary times, major mountain ranges were built, such as the modern Alps and Himalayas (pp. 46-47).

CARBONIFEROUS	PERMIAN	TRIASSIC	JURASSIC	CRETACEOUS	TERTIARY	QUATERNARY
PALAEOZOIC		MESOZOIC			CENOZOIC	
300 Ma		200 Ma		100 Ma	65 Ma	

Index

Acknowledgments

Dorling Kindersley would like to thank:
Henry Buckley, Andrew Clarke, Alan Hart and Chris Jones at the Natural History Museum; Ken McClay, Sun Professor of Structural Geology at Royal Holloway University of London; John Catt at Rothamsted Experimental Station; the staff at the Institute of Oceanographic Sciences Deacon Laboratories; the staff at the British Antarctic Survey; Brian Taylor and Fergus McTaggart at the British Geological Survey; BP Exploration for the core sample on page 27; Frances Halpin for the chemistry experiments; The Old Southern Forge for the iron on page 29.
Illustrations Stephen Bull
Photography Andy Crawford, Mike Dunning, Neil Fletcher, Steve Gorton, Colin Keates, Dave King, James Stephenson, Harry Taylor, Peter York
Index Jane Parker

Picture credits
t=top b=bottom c=centre l=left r=right

B & C Alexander 58b. Biofotos/Heather Angel 17tl. Bodleian Library, Oxford 9br; 9tr. Bridgeman/Royal Geographical Society 8tl; /Louvre, Paris 52tl. Oriental Section, Bristol Museums and Art Gallery 9b. British Antarctic Society 6br; 19tr; 32bl; /E.Wolff 19br; /R.Mulvaney 19bc; /NOAA 39br. British Geological Survey 6tr; 21br; 61tl. Bruce Coleman Picture Library /Jules Cowan 17clb; /M.P.L.Fogden 20 cl. James Davis Photography 50-51b. Joe Cornish 55l. John Catt 52r; 52bc. Mary Evans Picture Library 22cr; 24tl; 30bl; 30bc; 34 cr; 40tl; 60 tl; /Explorer Biblioteca Reale, Torino 8bl. ffotograff/Charles Aithie 50cl; 52bl; 56tr; /Jill Ranford 51tc. Greenpeace/Loor 18bl. Gwynedd Archive Service 28cb. Robert Harding Picture Library 37tr; 37bl; 39cla; 44clb; 47cr; 63cr; /Y. Arthus Bertrand Explorer 56cr; /Margaret Collier 56cl; /Ian Griffiths 50tr. Hulton Deutsch 31tl. Image Bank/Joanna MacCarthy 41cr; /H.Wendler 53tr. Institute of Oceanographic Sciences:

Deacon Laboratory 38tr; /MIAS 33tr. Impact/Martin Black 9bl. Japanese Archive 42tl. Mansell Collection 8cr; 8br; 18tl; 34tr; 46tl; 60tr; 62tr. NASA 6tl; 10tl; 11tr; 11tc; 12bc; 34br; 49tl; 49c; 57tl. National Archives of Canada 41tr; 62clb. National Maritime Museum Publications 30br. National Oceanic and Atmospheric Administration/National Geophysical Data Centre 36bl; 36tl; 37c; 37tcl; 37br. Natural History Museum Picture Library 13cbr. Image Select/Ann Ronan 22tl. Clive Oppenheimer 25l. Oxford Scientific Films/John Downer 49tr; /Mills Tandy 55br; /Konrad Wothe 46cr. Planet Earth Picture Agency/Peter Atkinson 10cr; /Peter David 32tl; Ivor Edmonds 59tr; /David George 24c. Princeton University: Department of Geological and Geophysical Sciences 38tl. Science Photo Library/Dr Gene Feldman/NASA GSFC 32c; /Mark Bond 26tl; /Tony Craddock 48c; /John Downer 37bc; /European Space Agency 1c; /Douglas Faulkner 38cl; /James King-Holmes 61cr; 61crb; /G. Muller, Struers MBH 29tc; /NASA 37tl; 45cla; 58cr; /Peter Ryan Scripps 38cr; /Soames Summerhays 45b; /U.S.

Geological Survey 37tcr; 43cra; /Tom Van Sant/Geosphere Project, Santa Monica 14tr; 18cl; 18c. Scripps Institute of Oceanography 32cr. Simon Petroleum 40bc. Frank Spooner Picture Library/Giboux Liais. 43cl; /Planchenault Front Cover. Clive Streeter 46clb; 54clb; 54br; 55tr; 59tc; 63c. U.S. Geological Survey 48tr. Susanna van Rose 29bl; 60clb. Vienna University-Institute of Geology 42crb. Alfred-Wegener Institute: Andreas Frenzel 35tr.

With the exception of the items listed above, and the objects from the Science Museum, London on pages 17cr, 12cl, 20tr, and those from the Oxford University Museum on pages 12rc and 62cl, the objects on pages 3tr, 4tr, 4tlc, 4b, 6tl, 14l, 15, 18/19c, 17bc, 17tr,17tl, 24b, 27tl, 27r, 29l, 33b, 41l, 41b, 43b, 46l, 46c, 46b, 48/49b, 53tl, 53b, 57tr, 57c, 56/57b,